The Homunculi Approach to Social and Emotional Wellbeing 2nd edition

of related interest

Cool Connections with CBT for Groups, 2nd edition
Encouraging Self-Esteem, Resilience and Wellbeing in Children and Teens Using CBT Approaches
Laura Seiler
Illustrated by Adam Alan Freeman
ISBN 978 1 78775 247 4
eISBN 978 1 78775 248 1

Having Fun with Feelings on the Autism Spectrum
A CBT Activity Book for Kids Age 4–8
Michelle Garnett, Tony Attwood, Louise Ford, Stefanie Runham and Julia Cook
ISBN 978 1 78775 327 3
eISBN 978 1 78775 328 0

10 Steps to Reducing Your Child's Anxiety on the Autism Spectrum
The CBT-Based 'Fun with Feelings' Parent Manual
Michelle Garnett, Tony Attwood, Louise Ford, Stefanie Runham and Julia Cook
ISBN 978 1 78775 325 9
eISBN 978 1 78775 326 6

The Mentally Healthy Schools Workbook
Practical Tips, Ideas, Action Plans and Worksheets for Making Meaningful Change
Pooky Knightsmith
Foreword by Norman Lamb
ISBN 978 1 78775 148 4
eISBN 978 1 78775 149 1

THE HOMUNCULI APPROACH TO SOCIAL AND EMOTIONAL WELLBEING

2ND EDITION

A Neurodiversity-Friendly CBT Programme to Build Resilience in Young People

Anne Greig and Tommy MacKay

Foreword by Rita Jordan

Illustrated by Rebecca Price

Jessica Kingsley Publishers
London and Philadelphia

First edition published in 2013
This edition published in Great Britain in 2024 by Jessica Kingsley Publishers
An imprint of John Murray Press

3

A CIP catalogue record for this title is available from the British Library and the Library of Congress

ISBN 978 1 83997 394 9
eISBN 978 1 83997 395 6

Printed and bound in Great Britain by Bell & Bain Limited

Jessica Kingsley Publishers' policy is to use papers that are natural, renewable and recyclable products and made from wood grown in sustainable forests. The logging and manufacturing processes are expected to conform to the environmental regulations of the country of origin.

Jessica Kingsley Publishers
Carmelite House
50 Victoria Embankment
London EC4Y 0DZ

www.jkp.com

John Murray Press
Part of Hodder & Stoughton Ltd
An Hachette Company

The authorised representative in the EEA is Hachette Ireland,
8 Castlecourt Centre, Dublin 15, D15 XTP3, Ireland (email: info@hbgi.ie)

MIX
Paper | Supporting responsible forestry
FSC® C007785

Contents

Acknowledgements 7

Foreword to the First Edition 9

Welcome to the Revised and Extended Edition of The Homunculi! 11

Part 1: Introduction to the *Homunculi*

1. Introducing the *Homunculi* 17
2. Theory and Evidence 23

Part 2: How to Do the *Homunculi*

3. The Nuts and Bolts of the *Homunculi* 35
4. Using the *Homunculi* Resource Bank 47
5. Getting Started 51
6. Carrying Out the Programme 55
7. Putting It All Together 63
8. A Whole Class *Homunculi* Project – Primary to Secondary Transition 71
9. Frequently Asked Questions 81

Part 3: The *Homunculi* Resource Bank

Carrying Out the Programme: Templates and Resources 91

Sample Cartoon 92

Blank Cartoon Template 94

Socratic Questioning 95

Mission Solutions 96

Agent and Mission 97

The Gadget Store 98

My Story Record: Beginning 99

My Story Record: Middle 100

My Story Record: End 101

Homunculi Template 102

Skull Template 103

Thoughts and Feelings Screen Template 104

Gadget Store Template 105

Traffic Lights: Stop! Think! Do! 106

Are Your *Homunculi* Working for You? 107

Whole Class Transition Project Resources 109

Activity 1: How Well Do I Think I Cope Now 127

Activity 2: What Do You Think Quiz 133

Activity 3: The What Happens Next Game 137

Online Resource Bank Contents List 145

References 147

Index 151

Acknowledgements

We would like to thank Ian who, at age 12, so impressed us with his insight, courage and originality. Without Ian, the adventures of *The Homunculi* would never have happened. Many other brilliant children and young people have taken part in *The Homunculi* over the years and each and every one of them has taught us something new. We have benefited from highly skilled and generous teachers who have implemented and evaluated the programme. We would like to mention especially Elspeth Davis and Kiersty Travers who helped us to engineer *The Whole Class Homunculi Approach* in Chapter 8. Kiersty's expertise in all the things teachers need to know in order to do *The Homunculi* helped in the production of specific teaching resources in this new chapter. Our colleague, Dr Amy Nolan, worked very hard supporting the delivery of our big transition project with Kiersty. We are also indebted to the many parents who allowed their children to take part and who celebrated their marvellous productions with us. It was Steve Jobs who said, 'The only way to be truly satisfied is to do what you believe is great work. And the only way to do great work is to love what you do.' To all of our helpers we would like to say that we have loved working with you on this fun and fantastic journey.

Anne and Tommy

Foreword to the First Edition

I am delighted to be able to write a foreword for this resource and that, at last, it is to be available to the public. I first heard Tommy MacKay talking about *The Homunculi* at a conference, soon after its initial development, and immediately recognised its potential. Here was something based on sound understanding of the psychology of learning and behaviour management and, even more unusually, based on an understanding of the learning style of those on the autism spectrum. Above all, it was practical and easily mastered by those working at the 'coal face', without necessarily having training in cognitive behaviour approaches or emotional counselling. Furthermore, it used attractive, child-friendly (indeed, 'person-friendly' – it appeals to the child in us all) materials and drew on familiar resources in most modern schools and homes. I knew then that it had great potential to help children and young people on the autism spectrum manage their lives and would also greatly ease the lives of those who work and care for them – often desperate to help but not knowing how.

I was so taken with the ideas and so sure of its value that I began to recommend it as a resource to teachers, psychologists and parents as I spoke at conferences around the world, only beginning to falter in my enthusiasm when it did not appear to be published. However, I should have taken more account of the scientific reputation of the authors. They were busy collecting evidence on its efficacy so that when it did appear, as now, users could be assured that it had an 'evidence base' in practice as well as in the soundness of the principles on which it was based. I probably needed to consult my own *Homunculi* to curb my impulsivity, but I am now delighted to give full rein to my enthusiasm.

The world of autism, of course, is not short of claimed 'panaceas' for the difficulties that often accompany the condition, especially in coping with the social world, including at school. Yet many of the promises far exceed the reality. Autism is complex and the problems occur at a deep level – not to be 'fixed' by simple behaviour management strategies. First order reactions of stress and anxiety lead to further issues of depression, low self-esteem and problems in behaviour management. Eventually these can become so burdensome that they lead to breakdowns in the mental health of individuals and/or in school placement. Once the spiral of failure has begun, it can be difficult to reverse.

The Homunculi programme can be started as problems begin, further pre-empting more severe difficulties; there is no need to wait until problems are deemed severe enough to 'merit' clinical help. The programme does not have to be confined to those on the autism spectrum as it will have much to offer a wide group of children and young people with developmental difficulties, and even those who are just struggling with life, regardless of the initial cause. It is a fun programme which uses skills that any educational programme would hope to develop. The teacher, parent or child does not have to choose between the academic and therapeutic curriculum: *The Homunculi* programme, like the best educational programmes, uses both. I have spent years advocating a cognitive approach to the education and care of those on the autism spectrum. However, I have often left it at the stage of principle, whereas *The Homunculi* programme takes it into practice. Now it is published, I will be even happier to recommend its use.

Rita Jordan, BSc, MSc, MA, PhD, CPsychol, ABPsS, OBE.
Emeritus Professor in Autism Studies, The University of Birmingham

Welcome to the Revised and Extended Edition of *The Homunculi*!

During the first decade of publication, a great number of interested readers, creative programme leaders and excited young participants have entered the magical world of *The Homunculi*. Or, as one youngster, Ewan, loved to call it, 'Homunc World'. There are many unique things about this world, but the one we love best is that it belongs not to us, but to those who are doing it, living in it, loving it and making it entirely their own personal creation. We are continually being blown away by the originality of those taking part and delighting in their suggestions for new Homunc World features. Indeed, it is their ideas and contributions that inspired us to revisit the programme, further demonstrating that Homunc World is a community to which we all belong and grow in.

A decade is, of course, a long time and brings many changes. The original members of *The Homunculi* community are now in their thirties and introducing their own children to the joys of Homunc World. Technology has super-fast forwarded and *The Homunculi* has burst into the online digital world quite effortlessly. Meanwhile, the actual world has been hit by an evolving crisis of poor mental health in children and teenagers as a result of the global pandemic, war and the soaring costs of living. There are also increasing numbers of children living with a diagnosis of autism as diagnostic services grow. Never before has there been a greater need for a safe place where the most vexed and vulnerable can retreat to and have the kind of fun that also kind of makes them stronger. We believe that *The Homunculi* is that place.

For all of these reasons, the 2nd edition of *The Homunculi* not only retains the structure for working with individuals or small groups of participants, it broadens its reach to much larger groups such as whole classes, units or even entire schools of children and young people. To this end, there is a whole new chapter on working with larger groups including teaching power points, lesson plans and curriculum links. There is a treasury of new photocopiable/downloadable resources including the brilliant movies made by groups of children going through transition to high school. There is a section on the change from analogue to digital materials, all beautifully illustrated in an astonishingly good video made by young Ryan. You can now also download and watch our teaching webinars on *The Homunculi*.

Below we outline what you can expect in the various sections and chapters of the 2nd edition of *The Homunculi Approach*.

In Part 1 we introduce the concept of *The Homunculi Approach* to social and emotional wellbeing and consider the evidence of its impact on children and young people, especially those who are on the autism spectrum.

In Part 2 (Chapters 3 to 9) we provide a systematic guide on using *The Homunculi Approach*.

Chapter 3 is a detailed explanation of all the nuts and bolts – things you will need to get started. This includes detailed examples of the characters and their missions and gadgets, the Skull poster and its key components (Thoughts and Feelings Screens; Stop! Think! Do! Alarm; Gadget Store), the use of metaphors, and how to prepare (e.g. location, working with parents and other adults).

In Chapter 4 we look at the Resource Bank – important materials needed to get started, according to the type and level of project chosen.

Chapters 5, 6 and 7 cover the eight steps of doing the *Homunculi*:

- Step 1: Meeting the *Homunculi*
- Step 2: Seeing the *Homunculi* in action
- Step 3: Identifying problems and missions
- Step 4: Pre- and post-project evaluation
- Step 5: Creating agents and gadgets
- Step 6: Deciding how to plan the story/mission
- Step 7: Story development
- Step 8: Debriefing.

Chapter 5 covers getting started, including how to use the materials provided to introduce the concept to participants; using the video links to demonstrate the *Homunculi* in action; identifying problems and missions. Finally, we discuss how to get the best out of the programme by a process of self-evaluation for the participants themselves.

In Chapter 6 we give a blow by blow account of how to create appropriate characters and gadgets, and provide examples of the type of dialogue that will facilitate those who may be stuck. We also describe the techniques that help to create good missions and story plots using a scripted approach.

In Chapter 7 we discuss the final stages of the project: putting it all together, including debriefing and detailed examples from our case studies and video clips.

Chapter 8 demonstrates a large group project by focusing on a whole class *Homunculi* project – transition from primary to secondary school.

Chapter 9 addresses some frequently asked questions – these have been greatly increased since the first edition of *The Homunculi.*

In Part 3 you will find a Resource Bank that can be photocopied or downloaded from library.jkp.com/redeem using the voucher code WEXCESQ.

These items include:

- an introductory sample cartoon strip for colouring
- a blank cartoon template for participants to create their own cartoon strip
- an information sheet for parents and school staff
- a list of Socratic Dialogue questions that can be used or adapted by therapists in guided discovery
- a Missions Solutions worksheet to help participants to come up with ideas for solutions to problems
- worksheets for the creation of Agents, Missions and Gadgets
- worksheets for the creation of story plots
- a worksheet with a template *Homunculi* character for participants who need further help creating their own characters
- evaluation worksheets.

Finally, Table 5.1 in Chapter 5 contains a detailed description of the contents of the video clips, to enable users to pick and choose which video clips to download and play for their own bespoke purposes.

In conclusion, in the 2nd edition of *The Homunculi*, we have endeavoured to bring to your fingertips the structure and resources you need to launch easily into your next Homunc World adventure. Whether it is to build up just one child or to set up a whole school or national *Homunculi* competition, or to create your own media platform to share or to design a *Homunculi* App, we have provided the tools to get you going.

Part I

INTRODUCTION TO THE HOMUNCULI

Chapter 1

Introducing the *Homunculi*

HOW IT ALL BEGAN

When (Tommy MacKay writes) my colleague Anne Greig asked me if I happened to know how she could get a copy of a cartoon strip from *The Beano* – 'The Numskulls' – I suspected her of having rummaged through my briefcase, for it just so happened that (for reasons best known to myself) I had the latest *Beano* there to hand. I asked her why she wanted it and she said it was for her therapy sessions with a 12-year-old boy, Ian, with whom we were working jointly.

Ian had been referred because of behaviour problems in the secondary school he had just started to attend. He was described by teachers as insolent, not respecting authority, having problems with his peer group and having poor temper control. When we saw him it became apparent that he had a wide range of other problems. He had difficulty with concentration, organisation and motor skills, and he was not making good academic progress. He was also scoring high on anger, anxiety, stress and depression and was at risk for suicide. He described himself as having no 'friend-making skills', and therefore no friends, and he was being bullied. He also seemed incapable of understanding the feelings or perspectives of other people. It was clear to us that Ian was a highly intelligent young man whose level of ability was masking undiagnosed autism spectrum disorder. We assessed him in our local autism assessment team and agreed on the then current diagnosis of Asperger's Syndrome. We then had the task of planning how we would support him in a school situation that was approaching breakdown and of devising strategies to address his depression and other problems of adjustment.

'The Numskulls' are Brainy, Blinky, Radar, Snitch and Cruncher, a group of little characters who live inside the head of a boy called Ed. They have the responsibility of making his brain work, but sometimes they are careless or fall asleep, and they like getting up to mischief. Sometimes, therefore, Ed's brain is not doing the things it should, leading to all sorts of problems. Anne's idea was to use this as one of the props in her sessions with Ian, combining the principles of cognitive behaviour therapy (CBT) with the use of cartoon strips.

I was intrigued by this and mentioned that for many years I too had used little characters – occasionally in my therapy work, but more commonly as a support for myself. When I faced a problem or a difficult task, I could call on one or more of a number of imaginary personae who would sit on my shoulder and help me to do the things I was not so good at doing myself. Each one had a name. For example, when I was sinking under a pile of unmeetable deadlines, I would say, 'Right, time for Speedy Gonzalez.' Suddenly I would be working away far faster than ever before. Or, if I walked into my study and could not move for disorganised piles of papers everywhere, I would say, 'Time to call in the Organiser.' Somehow things would then become a lot easier, and the task of getting everything into order would no longer seem insurmountable.

It was clear what was happening here. I was using a metacognitive prop. Metacognition means 'thinking about our own thinking'. By calling on an imaginary character who could think in a different way from my own usual way of thinking I was able to get a fresh perspective – to see things from a different point of view, through the eyes of someone who was good at doing the things that for me were difficult.

And so, from Anne's simple question and the discussion that ensued, the idea of *The Homunculi* was born. It combines two main fields of psychology: metacognition, allowing young people to develop fresh perspectives on their own thinking, and cognitive behaviour therapy, empowering them to change their thoughts and behaviour. Soon after, in Paris, we made our first scientific presentation of *The Homunculi*, a case study showing how in a very short space of time it was already transforming the life of Ian. We have since conducted extensive field studies involving large numbers of children and adolescents, as well as hundreds of presentations to road test the idea with thousands of professionals and others – *The Homunculi* is now available in a form that can be used by everyone.

THE HOMUNCULI: WHAT IT IS AND WHAT IT DOES

When we designed *The Homunculi* we wanted a programme that would be imaginative, interesting to children and young people, motivating, clearly structured and based on sound theoretical foundations. It had to be suitable for using in either individual or group situations and it had to be capable of addressing a very wide range of problems experienced by children and young people in their development. It is specifically geared to addressing the difficulties of young people on the autism spectrum. However, many young people who are not on the spectrum face similar issues of anxiety, depression, poor social skills or more general difficulties of coping with the demands of ordinary life in school, at home or in the community. We have found *The Homunculi* equally effective with a wide range of young people who are facing challenges in their social, emotional or behavioural development.

'*Homunculi*' is a Latin word meaning 'little people'. In practical terms, the fold-out picture of a head provided with the pack depicts a drawing of the inside of a skull that can flexibly contain, for example, an eye department, sleeping department, eating department or conference room. Children create their own characters and departments on the basis of problems they wish to solve. Each character is given a name and a job description or script of what they can do.

In our first case study with Ian, five main characters were created to deal with moods, sleep problems, friendships, communication and motor tics (Moody, Couch Potato, Gaffa, Chatterbox and Twitch, respectively). In terms of the job description or script, for instance, Moody helped him to stop shouting or being aggressive, to stop going into a bad mood and to stop hurting inside. Couch Potato helped him to get to sleep at night. Gaffa looked after facial expressions and also helped him to know when he should pause and let others speak. Chatterbox helped him to 'know when to stop talking, take turns, be interesting and interested'. The job of Twitch was to stop nervous twitches and jumpiness.

Special gadgets were allocated to each character: for example, Gaffa had a friendship repair tool kit. In addition, a Head Homunculus is in charge. It is his job to be always on patrol, to notice when problems arise by monitoring a 'thoughts and feelings screen' inside the Skull and responding to an early warning system of flashing traffic lights: 'red = stop; amber = think; green = do'. He also has a 'Good Rule Book' that contains advice about problems written in the form of social story scripts (for example, how to get a good night's sleep).

Therapeutic sessions involve working through a specific problem visually using relevant characters and an array of gadgets, located in the Skull 'Gadget Room'. Characters and gadgets are therefore detachable and can be moved to enact the problem story line visually. The child or therapist records the evolving story on a proforma. This provides a record of the session and can be used by the child later to create, for example, a cartoon strip as homework.

Importantly, the young people enjoy working on the programme, and so also do those who are working with them.

WHO CAN USE *THE HOMUNCULI*?

We have designed *The Homunculi* so that it can be used by anyone. There is a tremendous gap in resources to address the counselling and therapeutic needs of those who are on the autism spectrum or who have related difficulties. This cannot be left to the scarce availability of psychologists and accredited therapists. Materials are needed that can help teachers, support workers, professionals in many different specialisms and parents in supporting young people's needs. We have taken the view that training in the use of the programme should be enabling rather than restricting. Training is available to support the use of *The Homunculi* and to enhance the confidence and skills of users, but the materials are also designed so that the programme is accessible without training being a prerequisite for its use.

Our aim has been to make the programme as flexible as possible. We first used it with individual young people in weekly therapeutic sessions, but it has now been used with children in pairs or in group situations. At the start the focus was on the early teenage years, but we have now used it across the whole period of middle childhood and adolescence from about age 8 to 18 years. Participants in our ongoing research have had autism spectrum disorder, attention-deficit hyperactivity disorder (ADHD), non-verbal learning difficulties and a general array of social, emotional and behavioural difficulties.

We have also aimed for flexibility in how the programme is carried out. It is based on a clear set of principles and procedures that are present whenever it is used, but it is easily adapted for different ages and problems and also for different personality styles, both of the young person and of the individual who is carrying out the programme. We have designed it so that it is ideal for incorporating work on cartoon strips, role play and use of video recording, all of these features being widely popular both with the children and with adult workers. However, not all workers or young people have the same style and interests and so the programme has the flexibility to take account of this.

A special feature of this 2nd edition of *The Homunculi* is that we have introduced a full new chapter with ideas for setting up a whole-class *Homunculi* project. This will be of special interest to teachers and primary school headteachers who are responsible for preparing young people for the transition from primary to secondary school. It is thoroughly embedded in the curriculum, and in our research it has demonstrated its potential to be of benefit to all children and young people, while fully including those who are autistic or who have other additional support needs.

WHY DO WE NEED *THE HOMUNCULI*?

The Homunculi is needed for two reasons: first, the widespread nature of the problems it addresses not only across the autism spectrum but in many other children and young people; second, the lack of flexible resources that are based on sound psychological theory, which young people find exciting and enjoyable and which have an evidence base for their effectiveness.

The prevalence of emotional, social and behavioural difficulties in childhood

There is evidence that the difficulties many young people experience in their emotional, social and behavioural development are more widespread than previously recognised, and that the prevalence of these difficulties has been increasing. This increase is well documented and it has accelerated in recent years. Within a UK context, the number of young people aged 6–16 years with a probable mental health condition increased from one in nine (11.6%) in 2017 to one in six (17.4%) in 2021 (Newlove-Delgado *et al.*, 2021). Issues include anxiety, depression, anorexia nervosa and other serious eating disorders, and emotional and behavioural difficulties in general. These figures are reflected elsewhere in the world. Globally the prevalence of mental health disorders among young people in the 10–19 age group is estimated at one in seven (13%) (Global Burden of Disease Collaborative Network, 2022). Since 2019 an additional factor has been the mental health impact of the Covid 19 epidemic (Adegboye *et al.*, 2021; Lee, Cadigan & Rhew, 2020). These disorders lead to high levels of personal distress for the young people and families involved and they show continuity into adulthood (Rutter, Kim-Cohen & Maughan, 2006).

Only a small proportion of these children and young people receive any form of specialist help. Many do not seek it (Radez *et al.*, 2022), and for those who do seek it there is a significant shortfall in resources (House of Commons Health and Social Care Committee, 2021).

The gap in flexible, evidence-based resources

All of these factors – the widespread nature of the difficulties, the lack of available personnel and the gap in resources – highlight why we designed *The Homunculi*. Even where staff or volunteers are available to work with children and young people to help them with their difficulties they frequently lack suitable materials and methods that specifically address the issues in question. In presenting our work on *The Homunculi* to a vast variety of groups of teachers, parents, mental health workers and others we have become aware of the extent to which it is immediately seen as filling a significant gap in available resources.

One of the most frequent observations made on the programme is that both children and young people and those who are working with them become very enthusiastic about it because it is not only helpful – it is fun and exciting. The significance of this is largely self-evident. People are much more likely to engage with an intervention if they are enjoying it and look forward to their sessions with it. Indeed, a recurrent issue for us has been how to wean young people off the programme when the time comes for it to stop – they enjoy it too much to want to move on.

It is clear, however, that enjoyment is not enough. A good intervention programme has two other requirements. First, it has to be based on sound theoretical foundations. Second, it has to have evidence for its effectiveness. These two requirements are examined in the next chapter.

Chapter 2

Theory and Evidence

THE THEORY BEHIND *THE HOMUNCULI*

The theoretical underpinnings of *The Homunculi* lie in the related fields of metacognition and cognitive behaviour therapy (CBT). The implications of these theoretical approaches are then applied to our psychological understanding of the autism spectrum and the other areas for which the programme has been designed.

Metacognition

Metacognition refers to 'an individual's knowledge about various aspects of thinking' (Moore, 1982). It has its theoretical foundations in cognitive psychology (Vygotsky, 1978). It is concerned with people's knowledge and regulation of their own cognitive processes while thinking.

It is interesting that one of the studies of metacognition, while relating to the unconnected field of reading difficulties in children, had the title 'Mr Homunculus the reading detective' (Currie, 1999). This is about the only place where we have encountered the same term in the academic literature, and it illustrates one of the basic features of *The Homunculi* – the need for the young person to be able to stand outside of their own thinking, feelings and behaviour and to reflect upon it: that is, to think about their own thinking. 'Mr Homunculus' was the voice in the children's head asking them if they understood, telling them when to stop if necessary and generally keeping them on the right track. He helped them to monitor their understanding of a situation while it was still in process and to teach appropriate strategies if they were failing to understand. He was a stimulus and motivation to learn, and a mediator in the learning process. In terms of metacognition, *The Homunculi* serves a similar purpose in relation to a very wide range of mental health and other issues. The programme has developed a very structured and motivating way to mediate the learning of new patterns of thinking and behaviour.

Cognitive behaviour therapy

CBT provides the core methodology underpinning *The Homunculi*. Its central tenet is that 'people are disturbed not by things but by the views which they take of them' (Epictetus, 135 CE, translated Higginson, 1865). The focus of CBT is on how people think about themselves, the world and other people, and on how what they think affects their feelings and behaviour. Its rationale is that people's affect and behaviour are largely determined by the way in which they structure the world (Beck, 1963), and that their thoughts or 'cognitions' are the most important links in the chain of events leading to disordered behaviour and psychological dysfunction (Powell and Oei, 1991).

CBT recognises that people with psychological problems, including depression, anxiety, anger, difficulties with social interaction and maladaptive behaviour patterns in general, frequently show 'distorted cognitions'. For example, young people at school who see a group of their classmates laughing in the playground might normally take a positive view that people are having fun and they would like to join in. A person whose thoughts are distorted and negative might automatically assume that they are being laughed at and feel angry, hurt or excluded. Beck (1976) described a range of these 'thinking errors' that included a perceptual negative bias, blowing things out of proportion and seeing worst possible outcomes. The aim of CBT is to help the individual to be able to assess the evidence in a realistic way, to become aware of negative and distorted patterns of thinking and to replace them with ways of viewing situations that are more positive and adaptive.

This has clear relevance for young people on the autism spectrum in particular, whose thinking is already marked by narrow, concrete and stereotyped views. The majority of autistic individuals experience at least one co-occurring mental health condition (Lai *et al.*, 2019). Up to 65 per cent of adolescents with high functioning autism have clinically significant levels of anxiety, depression and anger (Gillot, Furniss & Walter, 2001; Green *et al.*, 2000). Their thought patterns are often very similar to the very rigid views frequently found in general among people who have depression or anxiety, for whom CBT can offer a means of developing new and more positive perspectives.

Psychological theories of autism spectrum disorder

In recent years there has been increasing interest in the concept of 'neurodiversity' in autism. Neurodiversity describes a continuum of behaviours and differences in people's skills, abilities and understanding. It enables people to talk positively about autism and to view it more as a natural 'difference' in thinking and being rather than as a pathology (Baron-Cohen, 2017). At the same time, for many people, autism is 'a severely disabling condition and the extent and severity of their consequent disabilities must also be recognised' (British Psychological Society, 2021, p.10). Perhaps the best approach to this discussion is to celebrate the differences found in autism in terms of special strengths and skills, in line with the neurodiversity model, and at the same time to recognise the challenges and difficulties autistic people face, in line with the deficit model (Kapp *et al.*, 2013).

In terms of these challenges and difficulties, our understanding of autism spectrum disorder is informed by four main strands of theory, each of which has its part to play in helping to explain the thinking, feelings and behaviour of individuals on the spectrum. While many other theories have been proposed (see Fletcher-Watson & Happé, 2019), it is these four that have formed the most enduring part of the literature on theories of autism since the 1980s. The first three of these are cognitive theories – theory of mind, central coherence and executive function. All of these seek to explain how the thinking processes of autistic individuals are different from the general population. The fourth, affective theory, is based on the idea that underlying the difficulties faced by those autistic people is a fundamental impairment in the realm of feeling, or emotion.

The Homunculi is designed to address the specific difficulties associated with each of these four theories.

Theory of mind relates to the ability to understand the mental states of others (Seyfarth & Cheyney, 2013). Baron-Cohen (1992), in applying this concept to autism, described the young people with whom he was working as follows:

> It was clear that these children were interested in people...but they appeared singularly oblivious to what others were thinking... It did not seem to occur to them that others might think them odd, or funny, or that others might think anything at all. (p.9)

People with weak theory of mind are likely to have difficulties in: predicting others' behaviour, reading the intentions and motives of others, understanding that behaviour affects how others think and feel, taking account of what others think and know and reading the listener's level of interest in what is being said; anticipating how others might react to one's reactions; deceiving or reacting to deception; sharing of attention; understanding social interaction; understanding pretence and differentiating fact from fiction.

Weak central coherence leads to a deficit in the ability to draw together diverse information into context, gist and meaning (Frith, 1989; Nuske & Bavin, 2011). It is a difficulty in seeing 'the bigger picture'. In his original paper introducing autism to the world, Leo Kanner observed this feature, describing it as an 'inability to experience wholes without full attention to the constituent parts' (Kanner, 1943, p.246). It explains the piecemeal style of autistic children in becoming fixated on detail rather than grasping overall meaning. While central coherence has been subject to critique as a general theory of autism (Pellicano & Burr, 2012), it is nevertheless recognised as having ongoing relevance to the difficulties found in autism (Walęcka, Wojciechowska & Wichniak, 2022).

Executive function (Ozonoff, Pennington & Rogers, 1991) allows goal-directed behaviour, problem solving in a planned and strategic way, flexibility in thought and behaviour, self-monitoring, inhibition of impulsivity and emotional regulation (Demetriou *et al.*, 2018). It is mainly associated with the development of the pre-frontal cortex, one of the key areas of the brain implicated in autism spectrum disorder (ASD) and a range of other difficulties and disorders. This part of the brain has implications which cut across all of the cognitive theories of ASD (Baron-Cohen *et al.*, 1999; Pellicano, 2010).

The affective theories (Gaigg, 2012) reflect Kanner's original observation that autistic children 'come into the world with innate inability to form the usual, biologically provided affective contact with people' (Kanner, 1943, p.250). They do not intuitively learn to relate through a built-in drive for what Trevarthen (1979) calls 'inter-subjectivity' – the need for shared experiences between children and their caregivers or others, a drive which is present from the earliest days of infancy. There is therefore impaired understanding of shared perspectives and impaired ability to use emotions to regulate interactions with others.

All of these theories have been subject to critiques. However, these critiques have been mainly at the level of demonstrating that no single theory has been successful in explaining all of the behaviours found in autism (Fletcher-Watson & Happé, 2019; Hill & Frith, 2003; Rao, Mysore & Raman, 2016). It is nevertheless recognised that each theory continues to make a significant contribution to our understanding of the issues found in autism spectrum disorder.

The Homunculi has been designed by psychologists who are committed to the belief that the best practice in helping children and young people on the autism spectrum or with similar difficulties must arise from a theoretical understanding of why they think and behave in the ways they do. It therefore sets out to address the difficulties that are associated with their specific issues and their likely causes.

It addresses theory of mind difficulties by allowing young people to stand back from their own thinking and find new perspectives that take account of the thinking and behaviour of other people. It addresses weak central coherence by building a reflective capacity to aid in grasping meaning, to build up the 'big picture' of how thinking, feeling and behaviour are linked and to generalise lessons learned into wider settings. It addresses executive function deficits by building structures for planning actions to achieve goals and by providing strategies to inhibit impulsive responses and regulate emotions. And it addresses weaknesses in affective function by helping young people to learn manually the things about emotion that come intuitively to those with typical development, so that they can build an understanding of appropriate responses to their own feelings and those of others.

The frameworks of metacognition and CBT provide the vehicles through which these difficulties and their theoretical underpinnings are approached. Overall, therefore, *The Homunculi* is supported by a relevant and comprehensive theoretical structure that provides a solid foundation for confidence in its use.

THE EVIDENCE: DOES *THE HOMUNCULI* WORK?

There are many programmes, treatments and resources for young people on the autism spectrum or with other kinds of support needs. These may be attractive and appealing, but often there is little or no evidence for their effectiveness. As psychologists we are committed to a scientific evidence base for all our work. It is not sufficient to know that we have a programme that looks exciting and innovative and is fun to use – or even to have good feedback from people who say, 'We have found this very useful.' All of these things are important to us, but we have to ask more crucially, 'Does it actually work?', and, if so, 'How do we know it works?'

This can only be done by careful case studies and field trials. In the case of *The Homunculi* we have approached this by asking two questions. First, is the programme based on principles and practices for which there is already an established evidence base? Second, is there specific evidence that the programme itself is effective?

Evidence: the underlying principles

In relation to the first of these questions, *The Homunculi* is based on two related fields of practice, both grounded to a large extent in cognitive psychology – metacognition and cognitive behaviour therapy.

Evidence for the importance of metacognition has accumulated over many years (Flavell, 1979). Metacognitive strategies are used very widely to support areas such as learning and problem solving (Marulis, Baker & Whitebread, 2020; Vrugt & Oort, 2008). There is also evidence of their central role in the treatment of specific populations, such as those with traumatic brain injury (Kennedy *et al.*, 2008). These strategies provide an established way to support children and young people in reflecting on their own thinking as a means of understanding and modifying their feelings and behaviour.

It is CBT that provides the principal foundation of practice underlying *The Homunculi*. CBT has a very strong evidence base, to the extent that it is recommended as the treatment of choice for several problems in the general population, including anxiety and depression (National Institute for Health and Care Excellence, 2013b, 2022). Its application to children and young people rather than adults developed later (Fonagy *et al.*, 2002; Stallard, 2002), but it is now recommended in the treatment of many childhood problems and is a first choice of treatment for children with anxiety and depression (Kreslins, Robertson & Melville, 2015; National Institute for Health and Care Excellence, 2014, 2019; Perihan *et al.*, 2020). In particular its use with autistic individuals has been developing considerably since we published our first paper in this area (Greig & MacKay, 2005). The evidence is pointing increasingly to CBT being an effective therapy for autistic individuals and related difficulties just as it is an effective therapy for the general population.

The use of CBT for children and young people on the spectrum is particularly appropriate because of the high level of co-existing conditions in ASD (Lai *et al.*, 2019). As CBT already has a well-established evidence base for dealing with anxiety, depression, obsessive compulsive disorder (OCD), anger, vulnerability to bullying and other issues, it is highly suited to dealing with such issues within ASD. Studies over the last few years with autistic children and young people have shown good results in areas such as reducing anxiety (Sharma *et al.*, 2021; Wood *et al.*, 2020), dealing with anger management (Factor *et al.*, 2019; Sofronoff *et al.*, 2007) and promoting daily living skills and independence

(Drahota *et al.*, 2011). The selection therefore of CBT to support *The Homunculi* was seen as a good evidence-based foundation.

The development of *The Homunculi* over two decades has incorporated from the start the key modifications to CBT approaches which are now recommended in the NICE Guideline on ASD (National Institute for Health and Care Excellence, 2013a, para.1.7.3). They include the following:

- emotion recognition training
- greater use of written and visual information and structured worksheets involving a family member, carer or professional as co-therapist to improve the generalisation of skills
- a more cognitively concrete and structured approach
- involving a parent or carer to support the implementation of the intervention, for example involving them in therapy sessions
- maintaining attention by offering regular breaks
- incorporating the child or young person's special interests into therapy if possible.

These are precisely the types of adaptation of CBT on which *The Homunculi* is based, and they greatly increase its appeal and effectiveness for working with children and young people on the spectrum. In addition to underpinning *The Homunculi* with these major fields of evidence-based practice, we have also incorporated many features in the programme that reflect ideas that are well established as making a valuable contribution in the ASD field. These include features of social stories and cartoon strips (Gray, 2015), which are currently being used with considerable success in helping to create a 'script' for the management of conventional social routines and for developing perspective taking; of Petersen's (1995) impulse control model; and of CBT-specific behavioural tools (Attwood, 2003).

The Homunculi also incorporates the concept of role play as a central feature. The use of role play and drama can make a significant contribution to addressing the challenges encountered in the autism spectrum (Sherratt & Peter, 2002). Social interaction and understanding are promoted through 'make believe' roles, which help young people to reflect on the behaviour and thinking of themselves and others. Language and communication skills are fostered by having a range of contexts in which to practise communication skills, to learn to understand non-literal language such as metaphor and sarcasm and to learn the importance of non-verbal communication such as facial expressions. Restricted and inflexible thought patterns are approached through the ways in which role play and drama have creativity and imagination at their core. Therefore, while the extent to which dramatic activities are incorporated or otherwise is fully adaptable to the personality style of the young person and the support worker, the underlying concepts relating to role play make an important contribution.

Evidence: the effectiveness of the programme

In relation to the second question, whether there is specific evidence that the programme itself is effective, the first research study for *The Homunculi* was a carefully conducted case study of a boy with Asperger's Syndrome who had just turned 13 when the programme started (Greig & MacKay, 2005). Presenting problems at school as reported by teachers included poor attention, concentration and organisation, inappropriate verbal and non-verbal communication and disruptive and attention-seeking behaviour. Other concerns as reported by his mother related to the impact of routine changes, sleeping and eating patterns, moods, tics, self-esteem and relationships. The level of his difficulties was shown in measures obtained in three areas: levels of depression, anxiety, anger and trauma using the Trauma Symptom Checklist for Children (Briere, 1996), social skills and competence assessments by pupil and parent (Spence, 1995) and observational school data in the form of teacher round-robin reports and assessments. These tests produced clinically significant scores for depression, anxiety, anger and trauma. Social competence difficulties were comparable to or worse than the scores obtained by a comparison group of young people with Asperger's Syndrome on the same tests (MacKay, Knott & Dunlop, 2007).

After ten weeks doing *The Homunculi* the results were dramatic. His mental health scores on the Briere scales are shown in Figure 2.1, with scores on anxiety, depression and stress all falling to below clinical thresholds. Social competence scores rose significantly, comments from teachers were transformed and in addition he developed the skills to establish a group of friends.

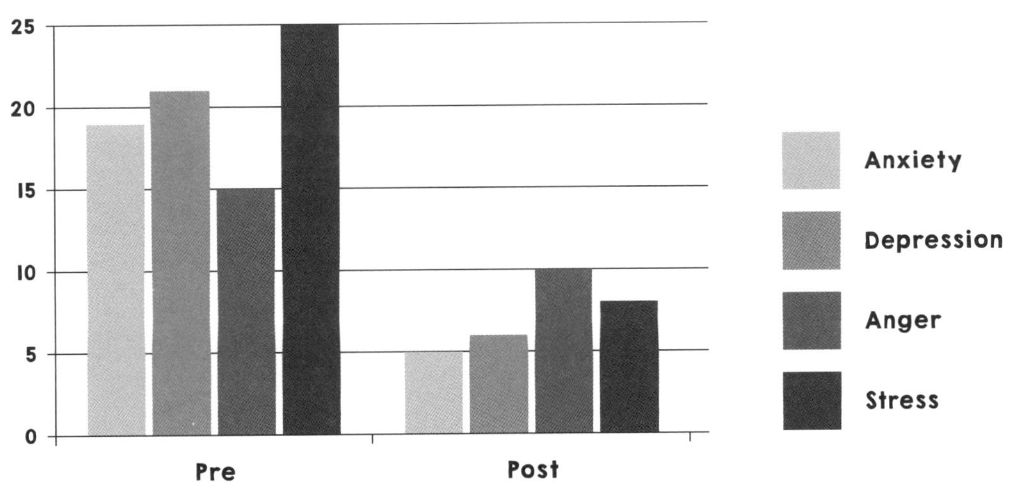

Figure 2.1: The first case study – improvement in mental health scores

Since this first case study we have used *The Homunculi* extensively in supporting children and young people in our day-to-day practice, and we have found consistently similar results. When we used the programme for groupwork with a number of boys with Asperger's Syndrome in a secondary school, the reduction in levels of anxiety, depression, anger and stress were very comparable to those shown in Figure 2.1, with corresponding improvements in other areas where they had been experiencing difficulty. This extension of the programme from use with a single young person in a one-to-one session to using it with a group was important in indicating that *The Homunculi* has considerable flexibility in the ways it can be used, and that it offers a resource for those who need to be able to work with several young people at once rather than working with children on an individual basis.

We have also carried out a further research study involving over 30 young people aged 8 to 18 years (MacKay & Greig, 2008). This was with a mixed group in terms of their additional support needs, with about half of the sample on the autism spectrum and the rest with a wide range of other difficulties. Specific issues raised by the young people as target areas to be addressed included exam stress, friendship problems, fighting and bullying, low self-esteem, swimming pool phobia, social confidence, inappropriate social behaviour, coping with change, anxiety and depression. Self-ratings on these target areas showed significant improvement, and again their scores on anger, anxiety, depression and stress fell considerably, reaching levels that compared favourably with general population norms (Figure 2.2). The statistical analysis of these results showed that they were highly significant and that a real change had taken place for these young people across all of these areas of difficulty.

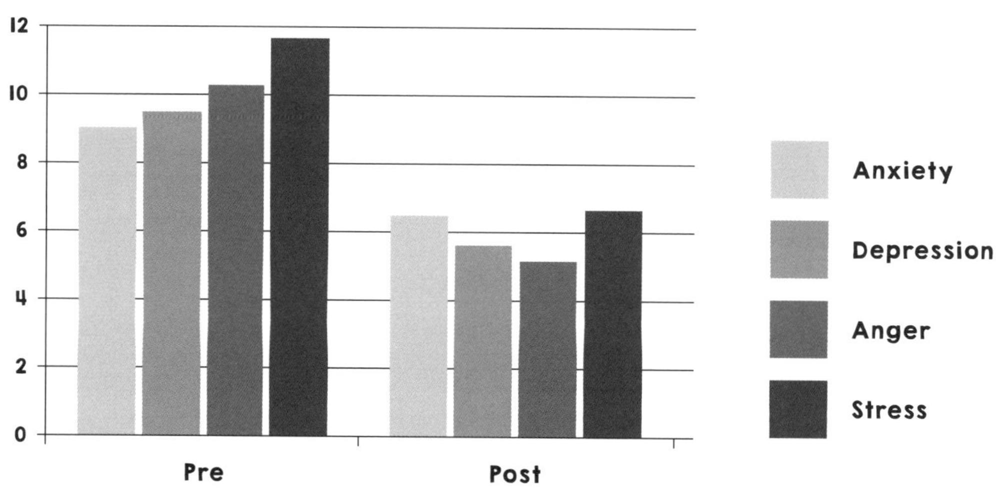

Figure 2.2: Mental health improvements in a mixed group of young people

These results are important in illustrating several benefits of *The Homunculi*. First, they show that it has been helpful not just in the case of one particular young person, but that when it is applied more widely it is also generally beneficial. Second, they show that the age range to whom the programme can be applied is also wide, as those who took part in this study ranged from eight years to the late teenage period. Third, they indicate that while *The Homunculi* was designed with Asperger's Syndrome in mind it is equally useful in addressing the needs of other children and young people with a variety of difficulties in their development and behaviour. These included children with attention deficit hyperactivity disorder (ADHD) and with a general range of emotional and behavioural difficulties. Fourth, the level of difficulty these young people had in relation to anxiety, anger, depression and stress, while clearly a problem that needed to be addressed, was not at the more extreme levels shown in our first case study in Figure 2.1. Sometimes it is easier to show a favourable result when the starting point of the problem is already at a very high level. The results of the wider study show that *The Homunculi* can also effectively address the difficulties that are less extreme but very commonly encountered.

We continue to develop the evidence base for *The Homunculi*, and in addition to our work with individuals and groups we have more recently extended the approach to whole class interventions in primary schools at the time of transition to secondary school. The philosophy behind 'universalist' approaches of this kind is simple. The best interventions for our children and young people with additional support needs are going to draw from the best principles we use with children and young people in general. Likewise, the best interventions for the general population will draw from our best practices for those with additional support needs. *The Homunculi* has been designed not only to address the clinical levels of anxiety and other issues found in autistic children, but also to support any child or young person with the normal levels of anxiety experienced in life in general.

With this in view we selected a time and setting which has traditionally been seen as a key stressor for children, the transition from primary to secondary school (Mackenzie, McMaugh & O'Sullivan, 2012; Rice, Frederickson & Seymour, 2011). We worked with an intervention class (23 children) and a control class (22 children). For the quantitative analysis the Spence Children's Anxiety Scale (Spence, Barrett & Turner, 2003) was identified as an effective assessment measure. This is a self-rating scale with 45 items relating to worries and anxieties, each of which can be rated on a four-point scale. To reduce the likelihood of a very short-term intervention effect of the programme, this measure was administered on two occasions almost a year apart – in the January of the transition year in primary school and in the December of the first session in the new school setting.

The results are shown in Table 2.1. Analysis of the scores before the intervention demonstrated no significant differences between the classes in terms of anxiety. After the intervention, the scores of the intervention pupils were significantly lower. It was also proposed that there would be differences between the intervention and control classes regarding their own perceptions of how well they would cope with the things about transition that worried them. Qualitative measures were devised using five-point self-rating scales covering worries such as being alone, getting bullied, peer pressure, falling behind with work and falling out with friends. The intervention pupils again showed lower levels of anxiety on the final measures (Greig, MacKay & Nolan, in preparation).

Table 2.1: Anxiety scores for intervention and control classes

Mean score	Intervention (n=23)	Control (n=22)	F ratio	Significance
Pre	31	28	7.216	p = 0.01
Post	23	27		

Part 2

HOW TO DO THE HOMUNCULI

Chapter 3

The Nuts and Bolts of the *Homunculi*

Figure 3.1: Homunculi character prototypes

THE *HOMUNCULI* MISSION

The Homunculi, which is Latin for 'little men' or 'little people', is a fun activity that aims to build social and emotional resilience in children and young people by teaching them how to think.

It involves a large, visual, interactive activity or game in which five miniature people (Figure 3.1) live inside a Skull poster (Figure 3.2).

The Homunculi are involved in great adventures and sometimes just ordinary stories too that are created by the participants to deal with their real-life problems. The Skull and its inhabitants are, therefore, an explicit representation of the inside of the participant's mind and the actual conflicts, dilemmas or difficulties they experience there. The little *Homunculi* are created to have specific problem-solving missions and special gadgets to help them, depending on what is happening in the real world outside the participant's head.

Young people love creating *Homunculi* characters and playing *The Homunculi* because it is about them, their life and the everyday problems that we know they have and that cause them stress. By means of their own creativity, we guide them through these difficulties in a fun, narrative kind of way that truly makes a connection with them, whatever age and stage they are at, and whatever other diagnosed difficulties they may have. It empowers them, gives them a voice and supports them in developing their own problem-solving strategies.

Playing *The Homunculi* is all about 'missions'. There is a 'big mission' and there are a lot of 'little missions'. Their big mission is to teach their players all about the way in which the thoughts they have are linked to the feelings they have, and the way they behave, when trying to deal with social problems. Then, when they are working in a particular story, they have a mission to solve specific problems, and the characters, from now on referred to as 'agents', each have a specific mission of their own within a story. The agents use certain gadgets inside the Skull. Other gadgets will be created by the young participants themselves.

In this part of the book, we describe the essential features of doing *The Homunculi*.

In the next chapter we go on to illustrate how to plan and conduct sessions.

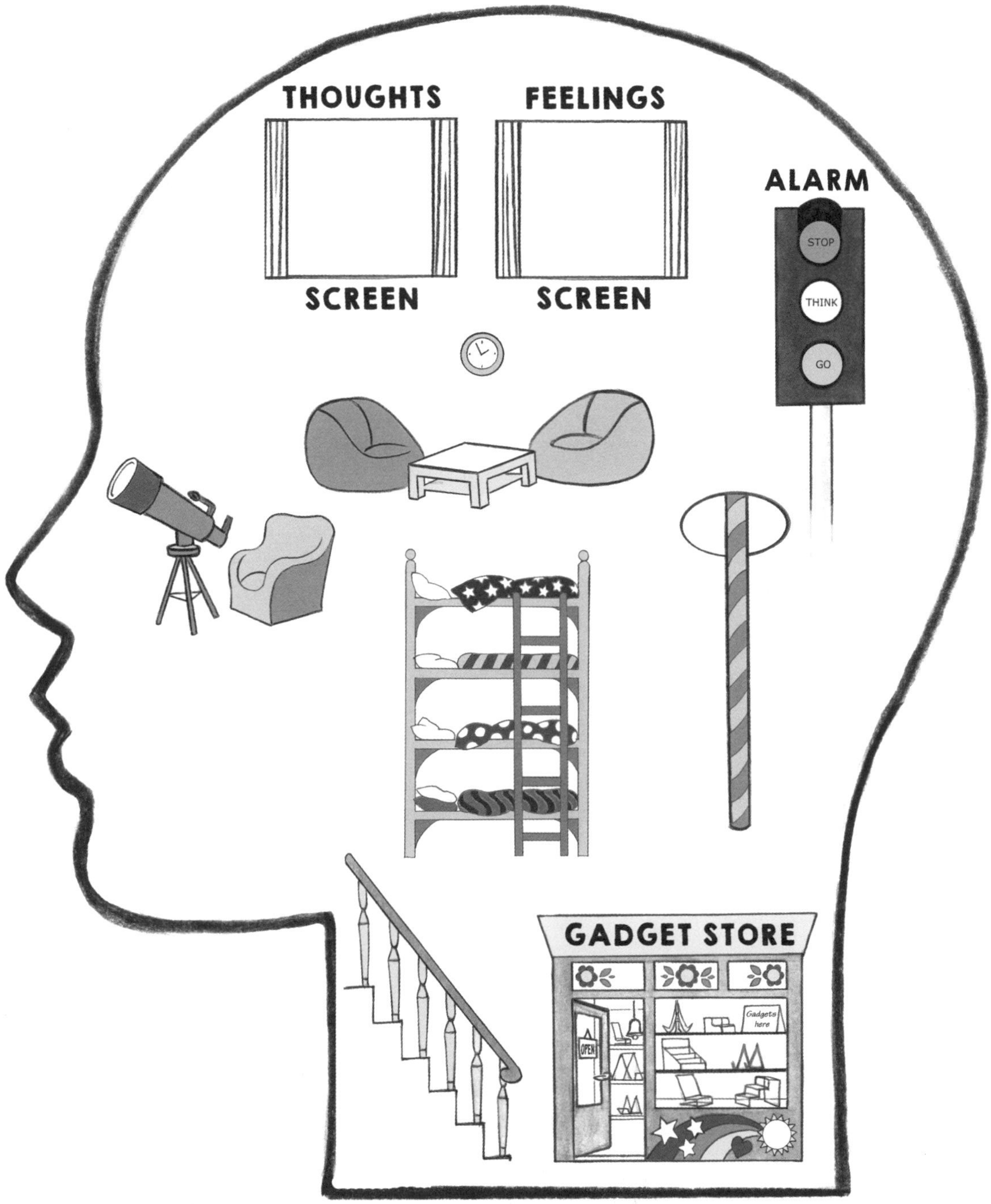

Figure 3.2: Skull poster

MISSIONS, AGENTS AND GADGETS

When young participants are taking part, the *Homunculi* are engaging in the most important of missions: to help them to master their own thoughts and enhance their thinking skills. The little agents created by the participants themselves will be showing them how thoughts, feelings and behaviour are linked. Big gadgets such as the 'Thoughts and Feelings Screens' and the 'Stop! Think! Do! Alarm' will teach them how to monitor automatic thoughts and feelings and to notice the effect on behaviour outside the Skull.

The gadgets created for the agents are showing them that thoughts, feelings and behaviour can be controlled, diverted, altered or completely changed. In addition, they are learning that a change in any one dimension such as 'thoughts' can completely change a feeling or an action.

Specific thinking skills that *The Homunculi* resource is imparting include:

- observation
- impulse control (learning to stop, think about things, make good choices, plan things and put them into action)
- perspective taking (thinking about the thoughts and feelings of oneself and of other people).

In designing their own agents and gadgets and using them to good (or not so good) effect in a problem scenario, participants are learning that they can effect change and that some choices are good and some are not. Figure 3.3 illustrates some actual *Homunculi* agents together with their problem-solving gadgets.

The characters in Figure 3.3 were created by two boys who wanted to work on their own separate missions but within the same story. One boy suffered nightmares, and the other struggled with making and keeping friends. The agents, gadgets and missions they created for this special joint mission were therefore as follows:

Agent	Gadget	Mission
Max Fax	A sorting hat to make decisions	Boss
Temperena	Magic gloves that release a relaxing image when rubbed	Anger control
Alexa	Friendship kit, breath-freshener to control speech	Friendships
Daisy	Tulip with purple dust; if sniffed, it collects up all the bad thoughts, which are then blown out through the mouth	Negativity
Pillow-walker	Dream-sabre that turns scary dreams into funny dreams	Nightmares
Wee Man	Magic word 'wee', helps him to get the right answer	Trainee

Figure 3.3: Homunculi characters

Further examples to help participants to create their own agents, gadgets and missions will be given later in the guidance sections.

THE AGENTS

If you are working with younger children, those with general or specific learning difficulties or those with a diagnosed psychological condition, you may find it helpful to start with three core agents as a rule and then allow them to create another two. These core agents have been created to ensure that there is a reflective structure built into the exercise to support planning, organisation, memory and problem solving.

The three agents proposed to fulfil this task are based on a basic metaphor of a learning hierarchy such as Boss, Manager, Apprentice, or Professor, Teacher, Pupil. This capitalises on the idea of a problem being identified, solutions discussed, with a resulting lesson, moral or cautionary tale for the 'pupil' or 'apprentice'. There are countless metaphors of this type that can be freely selected, the important consideration being that the chosen metaphor is based on the participant's interests and is salient to the problems at hand. This will also be highly motivating for participants. Some further examples of metaphors and associated agents used for imposing a preferred culture on the inner Skull are below. The first three of these examples tend to work better in terms of the effectiveness of the metaphor:

- The Skull is a ship (e.g. yacht, cruise, space, pirate) with Captain, First Mate, Ensign.

- The Skull is a social game pitch (e.g. football, hockey, baseball, netball) with Manager, Referee, Player/s in positions, Substitutes.
- The Skull is a Private Investigator agency (e.g. for the detection and solving of a crime) with Sherlock, Watson, Constable.
- The Skull is like a fridge or food cupboard (e.g. battles with food, eating problems) with Big Cheese, Cottage Cheese, Baby Spud.
- The Skull is the house of a girl band (e.g. for self-image issues) with Scary Spice, Sporty Spice, Baby Spice (or salient alternatives such as Moody Spice, Brainy Spice, Arty Spice, and so on).
- The Skull is a jungle (e.g. for sensory issues to do with sound, sight, taste, touch, smell) with Lion (King), Bat (ears), Wolf (smells).
- The Skull is a time-scape, such as prehistoric, inhabited only by dinosaurs (e.g. using a special interest) with any combination of carnivores and herbivores according to the task.

Practice has shown that it is not always necessary to stick to this formula as some participants find it too restricting. With simple direction from an adult or a skilled peer helper, the participants are still able to learn the important lessons of social problem solving inherent in the activity even if their preferred agents are random choices, as was the case with the two boys above.

However, children on the autistic spectrum or with attention deficits tend to benefit more from using the core agents as described above. Programme leaders may also find it helpful to use the core character for initial sessions during the phase of first getting to know how to do *The Homunculi*.

If the metaphor is used, the Boss's principal job is to keep watch outside the Skull, to raise the alarm and to make sure things are happily resolved. The Manager's main job is to motivate others and to keep track of the Apprentice. The Apprentice has to observe and state what lessons have been learned at the end of the story. If the metaphor is not used, any agents the child chooses can perform these tasks, although this is not always essential for learning to take place. Figure 3.4 shows some of the 'food' and 'jungle' characters created by participants.

Figure 3.4: Jungle and food Homunculi characters (continues)

Figure 3.4 cont.: Jungle and food Homunculi characters

GADGETS

Like all good stories, the *Homunculi* have some exciting gadgets to play with, the best of which are actually created by the participants themselves. The Skull is home to a number of essential big gadgets that are integral to the story plot development because they are designed to enhance participants' thinking skills. For this reason, the Skull comes pre-furbished with a set of featured gadgets. These are now described below.

The Thoughts and Feelings Screens

This device is depicted high up in the Skull in the forehead area (see Figure 3.2). This gadget creates the scope for self-reflection about the story problem: the *Homunculus* appointed to be the watchman in the Eye Department notices and describes the problem through the eyes. He then needs to go to the screens (see Figure 3.5) to find out what the person is thinking and feeling. The alarm summons the entire *Homunculi* team, who then have to suggest ways of solving the problems. The screens are revisited during the story plot and changed as the problems are tackled, and the story only ends when the screens have changed to positive statements. In the prototype, the screens were simply two pads of yellow sticky notes that could be attached and written on and discarded as the contents changed.

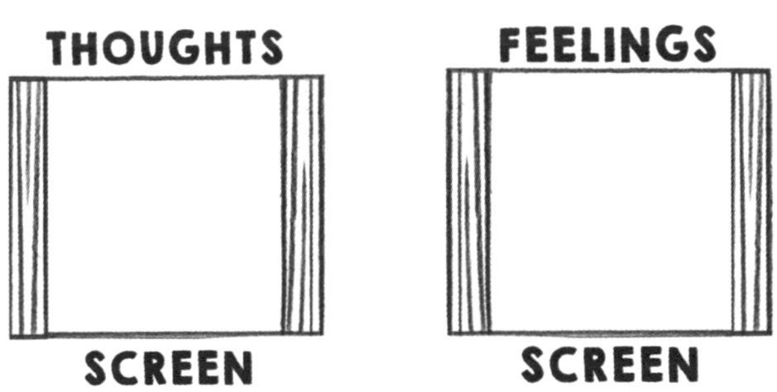

Figure 3.5: Example of 'Thoughts and Feelings Screens' using sticky notes

Figure 3.6: The 'Stop! Think! Do! Alarm' is connected to the 'Thoughts and Feelings Screens'

Stop! Think! Do! Alarm

This gadget is based on a cognitive and behavioural model for impulse control. It is depicted in the Skull template as a traffic light alarm with red for 'stop', amber for 'think' and green for 'do/go' (see Figure 3.6 for an alarm system). It is a metaphor all children and young people grasp easily. The participants can create their own sound effects for the alarm going off. The watchman will raise the alarm system in the same way in every story: the red alarm when the problem is identified and defined; the amber alarm when the agents are thinking about it and planning solutions; and the green alarm when the problem is solved.

Gadget Store

This is the store for the gadgets created by the participants for their agents to use in solving the specified problems. Participants can discuss and create what goes into the Gadget Store (see Figure 3.7). Depending on the problems identified, the store might contain, for example, gadgets for helping with relationships, for managing emotions, for managing negative thoughts and for managing behaviour (e.g. a friendship repair kit such as a mobile/cell phone to call and say 'sorry'; a card saying 'I miss you'; an invitation to a game or party; a Truth-o-Meter for weighing up the evidence for or against a particular decision, thought or action).

Figure 3.7: The 'Gadget Store' is located in the Neck Department

Figure 3.8 depicts some actual gadgets that have been created by participants. These feature a Revolter Jolter, that stops unwelcome negative thoughts, a Thought Reverser for when the negative thoughts get through to turn them into the opposite, a Calm-Ray Beam, which emits relaxing colours and sounds, a Magic Sorter Tray that organises tasks, and tins of Problem-Solving Paint, which allows you to paint dark things a rosier shade.

Figure 3.8: Gadgets created by participants for their own agents and missions

If the participant is stuck, the gadgets depicted in Figure 3.8, and indeed any of the figures, are a very good starting point for them. They can take the same idea and personalise it in terms of their own agent and mission.

THE BIG MISSION PLAN

The *Homunculi* programme should consist of ten one-hour sessions. This can be a flexible programme depending on time available. In most mainstream schools, one session each week over a ten-week period is the most usual as it will fit in with other learning commitments and the duration of one term (give or take a week). However, in other contexts, such as at home, during school vacations, in a specialist unit/school or in a residential setting, there are fewer restrictions in terms of time. In these contexts the programme would also work well over a two-week period with one session per day. Some sessions may entail homework or follow-up but it is important to avoid the programme becoming too intense. In the next section we discuss preparation for the sessions, and in the following chapters we give a detailed outline of how to do the programme.

PREPARATION

Working well with parents and carers

If you are working therapeutically with a participant or a group of youngsters, you are advised to consult with the participant's parents or guardians and to seek permissions. It is helpful to meet with them and show them the materials and an example of a relevant completed video clip. Older participants can give their own permission independently. However, unless this is a problematic area for the participant, it is helpful to involve parents and they can often provide good advice regarding the problems to be worked on and in feeding back about the success of the programme. If you are working creatively with participants for a different reason such as exploring technology and art projects, some information about *The Homunculi* for parents should suffice. A standard summary sheet of the concept of *The Homunculi* is included in Part 3, entitled 'Information for parents'.

The location

It is important to establish a good base to work from while conducting the *Homunculi* programme. A separate room for the whole duration is the optimal arrangement, especially for children with additional needs, as it provides less distraction, disruption and a good sense of routine and predictability for the participants. You will also need to discuss things the participants find difficult in their lives and they are due respect and confidentiality. If space is at a premium, some tasks such as the creation of agents and gadgets can be done in open areas or in classroom settings, so long as any associated discussion is private. If filming is involved, a quiet space is essential. Schools and other associated settings are noisy places and it will not be possible to remove all distractions. However, the aim is to plan sensibly to minimise potential distractions and disruptions.

Chapter 4

Using the *Homunculi* Resource Bank

The Resource Bank can be as simple or as complicated as you like. The package you go for will be informed by a range of things such as budget, availability of resources, time, access to technology support and the ability and preferences of the participants. It may help to conceptualise the programme as being operative at three different levels, depending on participants' needs and abilities and how these evolve at different stages in the programme (as shown in Box 4.1). Depending upon your preferred approach (comic strip, video clips or just talking), you will find an appropriate Resource Bank.

BOX 4.1

LEVELS OF DOING *THE HOMUNCULI*

Level 1

This Resource Bank will help the initial part of any programme but is also perfectly adequate if your participants wish merely to enjoy the process of talking about and creating their *Homunculi* characters and playing out what happens to them rather than going on to make a digital comic strip or cartoon out of their sticky notes board or worksheet cartoon. It is also the best approach where ability, time and resources are restricted.

Level 2

This Resource Bank is appropriate when participants are able to take the programme a step further and make a digital cartoon strip.

Level 3

This Resource Bank is appropriate when participants are able to go on to make a digital film (and perhaps also a digital comic strip as well).

The use of such technology is now quite common in most educational establishments and children and young people can come to the programme well practised in the use of real-life gadgets such as mobile phones, laptops, software, digital cameras and making movies.

However, if this is not the case, *The Homunculi* can still operate effectively at Level 1 with simple sticky notes aiding the storyboard development.

Box 4.2 suggests the range of equipment that may be useful at these different levels of engaging in *The Homunculi*. All levels will require:

- the Skull poster (you can find this in Part 3: The *Homunculi* Resource Bank or available to download)
- worksheets and templates from Part 3 (which can be photocopied from the book or downloaded from the JKP Library)
- video clips (also available to download from the JKP Library).

Not all of these items are required at each level. For example, it is possible to go straight to film and to bypass all other options such as comic books or strips.

BOX 4.2

MATERIALS FOR EACH LEVEL

Level 1: Doing *The Homunculi* without recording it

At this level, participants will identify their problem areas, create agents and gadgets, talk and play through a mission and story plot and may make a storyboard in words and/or drawings (see Figures 6.1 and 6.2). The following items are in this resource or readily available in most classrooms or care centres, so you just need to gather them together.

- Skull poster
- worksheets (e.g. blank cartoon worksheets)
- templates (e.g. blank character and tools worksheets)
- sticky notes in various colours and sizes
- vibrant colour crayons and pencils
- scissors
- Sellotape

- Blue/White Tack
- blank cartoon strip grids (for placing sticky notes)

Level 2: Doing *The Homunculi* and making a digital comic strip

This equipment may or may not be already available, and may involve ordering or borrowing some specific materials. You are most likely to need these if you are making a digital comic strip based on photographs. The use of cameras, downloading photographs onto a computer and applying a comic strip programme are well within the abilities of most participants from the upper primary stage. It may take a few extra sessions for training and completion at Level 2. However, programme leaders can also contribute to this if appropriate.

- all of the Level 1 Resource Bank
- digital camera (phone cameras work well too)
- computer to download images and software for the comic strip (e.g. Comic Life)
- photo animation software that makes still images move (e.g. Crazy Talk)

Level 3: Doing *The Homunculi* and making a digital video

- all of the Level 1 and 2 Resource Banks
- a camera for recording film
- a box with a range of things to help with special visual effects (e.g. things to make alarm noises, torches for lighting effects, slender sticks to attach characters to for movement, wigs, etc.)
- animation software (e.g. Stop Motion Go) if the film is to have actual moving characters

PLANNING THE SESSIONS

The ten-week programme has three distinct phases. These are covered in the next three chapters.

In the first phase, *Getting Started*, we cover the topics of introducing the concept of *The Homunculi* to participants, identifying problems and carrying out the initial evaluation.

In the second phase, *Carrying Out the Programme*, we cover the topics of creating agents and gadgets and of developing the story plot or missions.

In the third phase, *Putting It All Together*, we discuss debriefing and provide a range of case examples of *The Homunculi* in practice.

Chapter 5

Getting Started

INITIAL STAGES

You will already know quite a bit about the participants coming onto your programme and the nature of the problems they need to work on from discussions with others or from your own direct experiences and observations of them. Once you know your participants, and once they are comfortable with you, proceed as follows.

Step 1: Meeting the *Homunculi*

Introduce the concept of the *Homunculi* by showing the sample programme cartoon to the participants. This is included in Part 3 of this book, entitled 'Sample Cartoon'. This will help you to explain the idea of the little people inside the Skull in an accessible way. It is a black and white copy because some participants may enjoy colouring it in for themselves.

Step 2: Seeing the *Homunculi* in action

Show the participants Video Clip 1. This will help you to discuss the nature of the characters, what they look like, how big they are, their mission, how they are involved in thoughts, feelings and actions, the role of the alarm and so on. Finally, it helps you to invite the participants to think about a personal story, and likely problems, agents, gadgets and missions.

The short summary in Table 5.1 describes the contents of the video clips that are available to download – a series of videos which demonstrate all you need to begin the programme. Video Clip 1 is the most useful general introduction for beginning a project, but you may prefer to start with one of the other examples, depending on your client's difficulties, interests and goals. Clips 10–14 are whole class/group projects on themes of the anxieties surrounding the transition to high school. The subtitling in the videos is the participant's own work, so please excuse any typos!

Table 5.1: Video clips

Case example	Nature of participant's difficulty	Themes
Clip 1 1 boy, aged 13 (also depicted in the 'sample cartoon' in the Resource Bank)	Asperger's Syndrome and depression	Conversation Being bullied
Clip 2 1 girl, aged 11	Diet, confidence and relationships	Food Diet control Being bullied
Clip 3 3 boys, aged 14–16	Asperger's Syndrome 3a Introduction to characters 3b The film Stress City	Exams Coping with stress
Clip 4 1 boy, aged 10	Nightmares and making and keeping friends	Social behaviour, managing negative, angry and fearful thoughts
Clip 5 2 boys, aged 12 and 14	High functioning Asperger's Syndrome* (*This was the diagnostic terminology used at the time of this clip)	Anger management
Clip 6 2 boys, aged 12 and 14	Conducting sessions with boys with ASD	A demonstration of programme leaders working with participants
Clip 7 Ian, aged 13 and 16	Evidence (Asperger's Syndrome) 7a Ian aged 13 7b Ian aged 16	Interviews of one participant's initial feedback on the programme and its impact in the long term three years later
Clip 8 7 boys, aged 13–17	Evidence (ASD group)	Interviews with a large group of boys with ASD who took part in the programme
Clip 9 Boy aged 12	A care-experienced boy on managing anger towards adults, anxiety and keeping focused on tasks	The first film example of a participant using an iPad demonstrating creative work using apps and the internet
Clip 10 Boys and girls aged 11	Bullying	The first set of iPad films made by a class preparing for transition to high school. 5 production teams (of around 5 pupils in each group) worked on themes that caused children in transition worries and anxieties
Clip 11 Boys and girls aged 11	Getting lost	
Clip 12 Boys and girls aged 11	Making friends	
Clip 13 Boys and girls aged 11	Work is too much	
Clip 14 Boys and girls aged 11	Work is too hard	

Step 3: Identifying problems and missions

Help the participants to identify three to five real-life problem areas or situations that are difficult to manage. If your participant can only think of one problem to work on, this is acceptable as it may be possible to identify smaller problems within the one big problem. This is a good technique for helping the participants to compartmentalise the problem into manageable chunks and then to work on the most troublesome areas first.

Most of the participants will be able to identify a few areas they need help with, but if they find it too hard, you may gently guide them towards the areas already identified by others.

Box 5.1 illustrates possible questions to ask a participant who gets enraged on the football pitch and ends up fighting. The participant's response or possible responses are not noted here, but the idea is to pursue the line of questioning in so far as you need to in order to get the relevant information.

There is a programme activity sheet in Part 3, entitled 'Mission Solutions', to help you with this step.

BOX 5.1

QUESTIONS FOR IDENTIFYING THE NATURE OF THE PROBLEM

Problem example: unable to handle competitive social sports

'It's sometimes hard for you when you play football, isn't it? I wonder what is most difficult about that for you?' (Wait for response.)

'Is it something that others do?' (Wait for response.)

'Is it something that others say?' (Wait for response.)

'Is it a thought you have?' (Wait for response.)

'Is it a feeling you have?' (Wait for response.)

'Do you think we could find an agent to help with that one?'

'That's a good idea, isn't it? Now maybe we could find a good mission and gadget for him/her?'

THE 'WHERE ARE WE NOW?' ASSESSMENT

Step 4: Do they work? A pre-programme evaluation

Use the rating scales from the Resource Bank in Part 3 (entitled 'Are Your *Homunculi* Working for You? Before...') to get a measure of the participant's view of their own current coping (baseline evaluation). This scale should be repeated at the very end of the programme ('Are Your *Homunculi* Working for You? After...'). It is also helpful to ask other people who know the participant well to complete the same pre- and post-programme evaluations. This could be a parent and a teacher or a classroom or playground assistant.

Chapter 6

Carrying Out the Programme

AGENTS, GADGETS AND MISSIONS

Step 5: Creating agents and gadgets

Help the participants to manufacture their own three core agents (e.g. the Boss, the Manager and the Apprentice) and a further two problem-solving agents based on your discussion to identify participants' problems (Step 3 in Chapter 5).

If you are not using the core agents, your participants will need to create five of their own.

Having identified a problem area (e.g. football), the types of questions that help to develop the participants' ideas are illustrated in Box 6.1.

BOX 6.1

QUESTIONS FOR CREATING AGENTS

Problem example: unable to handle competitive social sports

'So you find it hard to cope in football because you think that the other players are tackling you unfairly. I wonder what type of agent would be good at sorting this kind of thing out?' (Wait for response.)

'What kind of people are involved in a football match?' (Wait for response.)

'What do they do?' (Wait for response.)

'What about different player positions? Does each player have a special job?' (Wait for response.)

If the participant is stuck, you can suggest some options as follows:

'Do you think an agent who is a referee or a manager or a coach or a player would be best to sort this kind of problem out?'

The preferred agent is then given a mission and a gadget specifically designed to solve the problem – for example, a magic football that floats in mid-air when something unfair happens, or a whistle that freezes the players in time. They can also use the standard gadgets (see Chapter 3). All of the agents created may relate to different aspects of one problem area or each agent may relate to a different type of problem. Encourage and discuss the use of different catchphrases and speaking styles for each character.

There are photocopiable worksheets to help participants with agent and mission creation ('Agent and Mission') and gadget creation ('The Gadget Store'), and a *Homunculi* template is included in the Resource Bank for the youngest participants or those with fine motor difficulties. Children who do not want to draw their agents and gadgets for any reason can download images from the internet (e.g. one pair of girls used a website called Paper Doll Heaven), cut pictures out of magazines or use actual photographs.

If writing is problematic, the participants' ideas can be scribed. The 'Agent and Mission' worksheet has a space to locate the drawing or cut-out of the agent and a place to write on specific mission targets (what the agent's job is). Scanning or photocopying the created agents and gadgets can be helpful in case of wear and tear and loss. It is then very easy to print off another copy.

Box 6.2 suggests a line of questioning to support the development of missions and gadgets.

BOX 6.2

QUESTIONS FOR DEVELOPING MISSIONS AND GADGETS

Problem example: unable to handle competitive social sports

Mission

'Ok. So when you are on the pitch, you think the other guys tackle you unfairly. It makes you really angry and you want to kick them. Often you do and get sent off.'

'What exactly do they do?' (Wait for response.)

'Do all the players do that all of the time?' (Wait for response.)

'Do you ever do the exact same things to other players?' (Wait for response.)

'Do you think they think they are playing fairly?' (Wait for response.)

'What do other players do when they get tackled in the way you described?' (Wait for response.)

'So what your agent (e.g. Referee) needs is a mission to freeze that moment in time when you have just been tackled and then to stop you from blowing up. His mission is to give you time to think through what has happened before you jump to the conclusions.'

Gadget

'What kind of gadget do you suppose would have such a capability?' (Wait for response.)

'What sort of things are always on the football pitch?' (Wait for response.)

'What about a ball, whistle or football boots?' (Wait for response.)

'If it were a magic whistle – how could it help with the mission?' (Wait for response.)

'So maybe it's a magic whistle that stops play by freezing it in time?'

or

'Maybe the noise the whistle makes sends a signal to the *Homunculi* that you are about to blow up and they need to stop you?'

Video Clip 6 illustrates the conversational exchange between the participants and project manager. The conversation shows how to develop characters, their jobs and gadgets and how to develop a more focused understanding of the problem and how it relates to the created characters.

TECHNIQUES FOR MISSION MANAGEMENT

Step 6: Deciding how to plan the story/missions

Your participants now have their own agents and gadgets. They also have a good idea of the problem areas to be worked on. The next task is to put them into a story plot, which will be their 'mission'. Younger or less able participants will need to plan the whole mission before they start filming. Some older participants or those with exceptional skills may want to make the story up as they go along. As a general rule, however, the programme is more efficient when a 'storyboard' technique is used. Various techniques have been used for this:

- *Option 1*: Sticky notes stuck on to a big sheet of paper, card or board. Each sticky note functions as a snapshot of what is happening in the story at that time. This looks like a cartoon strip, but has the flexibility of just writing words or just making sketches on each sticky note. As sticky notes come in different colours and sizes, they too can be used creatively to mark different episodes. Bits can also be moved around or thrown away. Figures 6.1 and 6.2 illustrate such a 'storyboard' technique.

Figure 6.1: Example of a storyboard technique using sticky notes

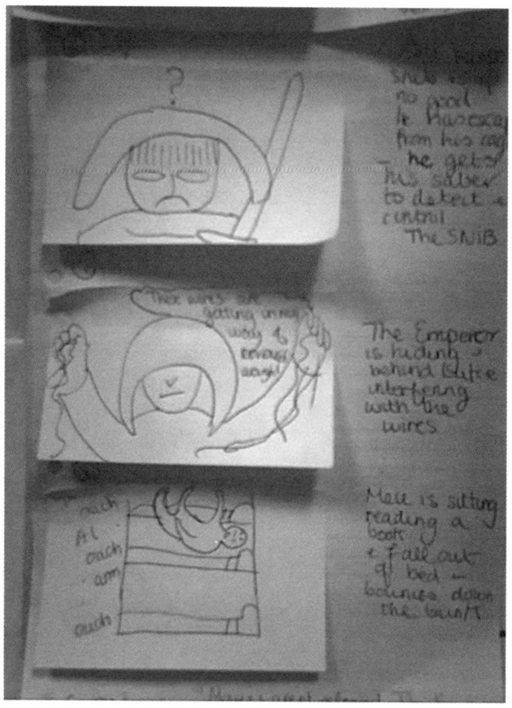

Figure 6.2: Close-up of a storyboard technique using sticky notes

- *Option 2*: A blank cartoon template is simply a blank page for the participants to draw and/or write up the sequence of events on. An example is in the photocopiable Resource Bank, entitled 'Blank Cartoon Template'.
- *Option 3*: Using software such as Comic Life. This requires digital photographs to be taken, downloaded and then put into a comic book format. For this approach, participants would need to act out the scenes visually for the purpose of taking

digital stills of the relevant parts to the story development. This is also a good alternative for participants who are unable or unwilling to use a video camera and it is easy to take pictures of the characters in various situations inside the Skull.

Step 7: Story development

With the above agents, gadgets, missions and a preferred story format in place, the story now needs to be developed along specific lines. It is important to follow the general formula for story development. It has been designed to provide a rule-based or scripted approach to tasks that is supportive of children who have planning, memory and organisational problems. It also ensures the use of key features of the programme that incorporate the principles of cognitive behaviour therapy (CBT) such as the 'Thoughts and Feelings Screens' and the 'Stop! Think! Do! Alarm' (see Figures 3.5, 3.6 and 3.7). Although there is a general script, there is plenty of scope for creative contributions from individual participants. The general scripted story plot means that each mission always starts the same way, always is developed in the middle in the same way and always finishes in the same way. The general script is as follows.

Start of the story

- The Boss is monitoring outside the Skull in the Eye Department. He/she notices a problem outside the Skull.
- The RED alarm is raised, which means it's time for the *Homunculi* to STOP what they are doing and report to the Brain Department.
- The *Homunculi* assemble in the Brain Department and the Boss reads out the Thoughts and Feelings Screens. The *Homunculi* mission is stated.
- (If you are using the Boss, Manager and Apprentice metaphor.) The Manager locates the Apprentice character to ascertain what he/she has been up to. He/she may be hiding and need to be brought in and have lessons to learn.

Middle of the story

- The alarm moves on to AMBER, which means time to THINK.
- Each agent has to give an opinion on what is wrong and consider whether or not they can help and which gadget they could use to solve the problem.
- One solution is funny but ineffective (having the Expander tool on the wrong setting and enlarging the characters); one makes it worse (using a hammer to hit the Boss's head); and one is a big success (using a mobile phone to get in touch with Aspie Hunter).
- Every time a new solution is tried, the Thoughts and Feelings Screens are changed

and consulted. Box 6.3 gives further guidance on using the Thoughts and Feelings Screens.

End of the story

- The alarm moves on to GREEN, which means time to DO.
- The Boss congratulates the solver and the lesson learned is stated both inside and outside the Skull.
- The mission is accomplished. They all celebrate.

BOX 6.3

USING THE 'THOUGHTS AND FEELINGS SCREENS'

The thoughts identified at the time of noticing the problem should be negative self-statements such as:

'I am worthless'

'I am stupid'

'Everybody hates me', etc.

The feelings identified at the time of noticing the problems should be negative emotions such as 'anger', 'despair', 'hate', 'fear' and so on, as in:

'I am angry'

'I hate everybody'

'I am afraid', etc.

When the *Homunculi* use an agent and a gadget that does not work, for example getting the Deflator Button stuck on reverse so that instead of reducing the size of the problem it makes it bigger, then an escalation in the negativity of the thoughts and feelings should be noted at that time. So a statement of:

'I am stupid' may then become 'I am worse than stupid – I am brainless'.

'I am angry' becomes 'I am raging'.

This teaches participants that anger and feelings are relative values that go up and down a scale depending on the thoughts we have. It also creates opportunities to teach them about the differences between anger and hate and other feelings as young participants can often confuse them.

When an agent and gadget have done a good job, alter the screens to reflect the positive change. In this situation the new thoughts and feelings are realistic, balanced and manageable:

'I am stupid' becomes 'I am as smart as most people'.

'I am raging' becomes 'I feel more relaxed as the problem seems much smaller now'.

'Nobody likes me' becomes 'There are some people who seem to like me and some who don't but very few who actually hate me'.

Please note these examples are not prescriptive. It is the idea of scaling and restoring objective balance that is important in changing the Thoughts and Feelings Screens. The use of role play to understand scaling is shown in Video Clips 3b, 4 and 5.

The worksheets in Part 3 show a number of special questions that are in the cognitive behavioural tradition of Socratic Dialogue and social problem solving, 'Socratic Questioning'. This will be a familiar approach to programme leaders with a therapeutic background, but they are easy for anyone to use. When a participant's thoughts are stuck, biased, blown out of proportion or lacking an evidence base, using such a format of questions takes the participant through a gentle course of guided discovery. These types of questions help children to explore their own thoughts and to restore balance and perspective to them. This is a thinking skill that will be learned in interaction with the programme leader. This social problem-solving activity sheet helps participants to plan options for developing their mission. It is designed to help them map out their thoughts, consider options, what the likely outcomes are in each case ('If...then...') and to make good choices.

Chapter 7

Putting It All Together

FINAL STAGES

Step 8: Debriefing

When your participants' story is complete at any level, it is good practice to obtain a measure of outcomes. It is therefore time to revisit the rating scales used at the start of the programme ('Are Your *Homunculi* Working for You?'). When they have been redone and compared with the initial ratings you can then discuss the evident progress with the participants and with others such as parents, carers or support staff who may also have contributed to the pre-programme assessment. Presenting the results graphically to the participants is often motivating and helpful as they will respond to the good visual effects of seeing their own measures dramatically improve.

Your discussion can go beyond rating scales to include more general feedback. This is especially useful when, for whatever reason, the programme has not gone as well as you had anticipated. You might include questions such as:

- 'What did you like best and why?'
- 'What did you not like and why?'
- 'What part was the most helpful to you?'
- 'What part was the least helpful to you?'
- 'Are there bits you found too hard? Why?'
- 'Who is your favourite agent and why?'
- 'What is your favourite gadget and why?'
- 'What would you do differently the next time?'

- 'If I were doing this with another person, what advice would you give me to improve it?'

Where a number of individuals or groups of participants have taken part in one area or setting, an awards ceremony like the Oscars can be arranged (e.g. best story plot, best devices, etc.). Otherwise, certificates can be issued.

Working with larger groups of children is described in detail in Chapter 8.

FROM THE CASE FILES

We now present a number of case examples. All items featured in this section are cartoons, clips and videos that have been made by the children who participated in various *Homunculi* programmes. The actual cartoons produced by the participants are available to download from the JKP Library.

Table 5.1 in Chapter 5 describes the contents of the video clips that are available to download.

CASE EXAMPLE 1: IAN (SEE VIDEO CLIP 1)

Ian was 13 at the point of both referral and diagnosis and was very low after two traumatic school transitions in a row. He found all aspects of school social life extremely challenging and stressful. He identified several missions for his *Homunculi*: dealing with his negative moods, feeling lethargic, getting along with others, making conversations and nervous twitches. In addition he was struggling to come to terms with his diagnosis, and his way of dealing with this was to do battle with it. Ian created the following *Homunculi* agents to accomplish his missions:

Gaffa: A kindly boss who gets on with everyone.

Couch Potato: An agent who never sleeps at night so is very lazy the next day.

Moody: An agent who deals with emotions, sometimes happy, sometimes sad, and has a two-sided face, one for each emotion.

Chatterbox: An agent who helps him to know when to take turns, pause, to say interesting things and to be interested in others.

Twitch: A nervous agent who hides behind the others and gets nervous twitches.

In addition, Ian wanted to directly address his diagnosis by inventing an agent called Aspie who created havoc inside his Skull. To deal with this miscreant, he created an Aspie Hunter whose job it was to sniff him out and get him under control. It is not normally recommended that a war-like metaphor is used but, in this case, it was where the young person was at and he would clearly find it helpful to work it through. In the course of many sessions, and several different mission stories, this approach created opportunities to discuss the nature of Asperger's Syndrome (AS) through psycho-education, and finally saw Ian progressing on to missions in which his agents were able to harness his talents that are part of his Aspie character.

Ian's story begins with him thinking he has just been pushed at school. While there were times this happened as part of teasing, often the scale of things was a problem of his interpretation in which an accidental bump escalated to murderous intent on the part of the bumper. Ian's very first mission for his *Homunculi* then was to get Aspie under control and into proportion. It is a very simple plot that does not fully exploit all of the *Homunculi* features but it is included here because it was the prototypical story that so beautifully illustrates how young people can intelligently identify those dimensions of having AS that are universally problematic for the group. Aspie is intent on blowing things up out of proportion using a bomb. Meanwhile, Ian's agents are trying out their own plans, one that's funny, one that makes things worse and one that does the trick and which will allow the rest of the *Homunculi* to regain control and get things back in proportion. Aspie Hunter arrives and saves the day.

CASE EXAMPLE 2: CHANTELLE (SEE VIDEO CLIP 2)

Chantelle was an 11-year-old girl showing signs of depression and social withdrawal at school. She felt unable to trust her peers. There had been some incidents of bullying and unkind teasing in the playground, feeding insecurities about her weight. One boy in particular was very nasty to her. Having agreed on a mission, she decided her characters would be food people (see Figure 3.4), who, according to the metaphor, became Big Cheese (Boss), Baby Spud (Apprentice) and a number of Managers, some of whom were good food and some bad – BLT the Burger (tempts her when stressed); Rosie the Apple (keeps her healthy); Cottage Cheese (mops up the mess); Madame Chocolat (vain and attention seeking but makes her feel good); and Bananas (a miscreant who makes things worse).

Chantelle chose to make a digital film of the cartoon, but was not happy to appear on film. She was an excellent artist and drew the scenes outside of the Skull. The mission for her *Homunculi* was to improve her self-esteem and will power in managing her diet and preventing her from feeling hurt by the cruel words of others.

Her story begins when the bully teases her by making up a cruel poem about her: 'She's fat, she's round, she bounces on the ground.' She cries and the *Homunculi* alarm is raised by Big Cheese. Bananas is creating chaos by setting a fire and melting Big Cheese, BLT thinks she should have some burgers because junk food makes her feel better. Chocolat is in league with him. Cottage Cheese is the practical one who holds it all together. Rosie thinks she can be more helpful with exercise. Meanwhile Spud is upset by all the noise. It is some time before her thoughts and feelings become balanced and positive and it is finally thanks to Rosie who uses a deflector device in her ear so that any bad words that come from others would be deflected back at them.

CASE EXAMPLE 3: STRESS CITY (SEE VIDEO CLIPS 3A AND 3B)

Three teenage boys with Asperger's Syndrome (AS), who were aware of their diagnosis, decided they wanted to work collectively on the shared anxiety of exam stress as they were about to sit their Standard Grades. They chose to create a digital video of a cartoon with real role play with themselves acting as the various characters outside the Skull. The boys created at least one character each. They created the following core characters using the metaphor of Boss, Manager and Apprentice:

- Boss (Miss Malcolm – based on their respect for the Principal Teacher of Support for Learning at their school). Catchphrase: 'Don't make me come down there.'
- Apprentice (Aspie – based on those aspects of AS that elevate anxiety such as disorganisation, problems with writing, anger and distraction through interests in other obsessions). There would be a small Aspie, a normal Aspie and a big Aspie who would change size in relation to anger and getting things out of proportion. He had three different tones of voice from squeaky to deep. Catchphrase: 'Oh no, I think I am about to expand.'
- Manager (macho character called Tracker). He has an Aspie Tracking Device and an Expander and Reducer which can be used to get Aspie back in proportion.

They created the following problem-solving characters:

- Coach (he gets things moving, works against laziness). Catchphrase: 'Get working, one...two...three...four.'
- Dr Spex (he is studious and thinks and plans a lot). Catchphrase: 'Now I'm going to have to think about that one.'
- Miss Hypno (she is in charge of relaxation). Catchphrase: 'Let me cast a relaxation spell – relax, relax, r-e-l-a-x.'
- B-Trayal (he is in charge of sorting out truth and lies). Catchphrase: 'It's so tacky!'

They developed the following story plot, opting for role play outside the Skull and narrative:

- The owner of the Skull is called Dom (made up of the names of all the participants).

- He is presented with a surprise Maths test by Mr Shocks, the Maths teacher.
- He panics, gets angry and tears up the test paper.

Meanwhile, inside the Skull...

- Aspie is getting out of proportion and creating havoc.
- The Tracker locates him.
- The Team is called and suggest options and gadgets. The Expander and Reducer are suggested to get Aspie back in proportion.

Meanwhile, outside the Skull...

- Mr Shocks makes him do the test with another boy.

Meanwhile, inside the Skull...

- B-Trayal makes him think of cheating in the exam just to get him through it.
- Havoc still reigns as they try to control Aspie.
- The wrong setting is on and they enlarge Aspie even further rather than shrink him.

Meanwhile, outside the Skull...

- Dom is caught cheating.
- He is reprimanded and sent outside to think.

Meanwhile, inside the Skull...

- The Tracker now has Aspie under control.
- The Boss confronts B-Trayal for making things worse.
- The lessons are stated.

Meanwhile, outside the Skull...

- Dom has had time to reflect about his cheating and damage to his friendship.
- He resolves how to cope better with exam stress in the future and apologises.

CASE EXAMPLE 4: ALI AND LIAM (SEE VIDEO CLIP 4)

Ali and Liam were classmates, both with big personalities. Ali had a diagnosis of dyspraxia and associated planning difficulties, together with general anxiety issues that manifested themselves in recurring nightmares. Liam had considerable dramatic flair but some of his peers found him over the top. His high levels of language ability also set him apart from his peers in terms of interest and conversational style. Having identified those troublesome aspects of their lives that they would most like to include in their joint *Homunculi* mission, they each created an array of agents and gadgets and a loose story plot. The boys were less interested in doing a comic strip or storyboard than other children as they both had a flair for role play. These boys were therefore comfortable to go straight for the movie, following their loose story plot and improvising. This would not necessarily be recommended for all children but it worked well for these two. The agents they finally used are depicted in Figure 3.3.

Their story began with Ali (aka Liam as they changed the names of their characters: Ali to David and Liam to Ali) getting into trouble with David (aka Ali) because he was saying 'inappropriate' things that were not found to be as funny as he thought. The *Homunculi* are alerted to the approaching trouble. Next Liam bumps into Ali and is not very apologetic. The Boss, Max Fax, calls a meeting and consults the Thoughts and Feelings Screens. It is not good news. He then puts on his 'Sorting Hat', which helps him to decide which agent should be used for the mission. He settles on the Anger Agent, Temperena. She has a pair of magic gloves that, if she rubs them together, will give Ali a 'relaxing image'. However, no sooner has she got to work than there is a short circuit and an explosion. Things escalate outside the Skull. Luke Pillow-Walker then uses his Dream-sabre to put Ali to sleep while they fix the problem. Alas, he is having a nightmare that there is a Kung Fu war at school and Ali is getting hurt. Luke journeys off via the ear tunnel to locate the dream and use his Dream-sabre to turn all the bad guys in the dream into funny guys. It works and Ali is laughing in his sleep and his nightmares are gone completely. Max Fax asks a different agent to make sure he does not blow it again and Alexa suggests her magic breath freshener that makes Ali say cool and nice things to his friends. When Ali wakes he finds David and gets off to a good start, but then blows it by telling him a bad joke. The Thoughts and Feelings Screens show hopelessness and despair. The *Homunculi* then bring in Daisy who has a magic tulip with purple pollen that, when it is breathed in through the nose, goes into the mind and collects up all the bad thoughts and takes them out through the mouth. This final attempt works and Ali and David (aka Liam and Ali) patch up their differences.

CASE EXAMPLE 5: ALEX AND BENJI (SEE VIDEO CLIP 5)

Alex has Asperger's Syndrome (AS) and is already an experienced 'Homunculer'. Benji has high functioning autism and is currently experiencing irrational outbursts of anger both at home and at school. Benji's mother has become concerned about his overt angry outbursts directed at her. His teachers have also noticed anger and increased swearing.

Benji's intense interest is football. This is used as the appropriate metaphor and he creates the following characters:

1. The Manager (Sir Alex Ferguson)
2. The Referee
3. The Coach
4. The Defender
5. The Striker.

His gadgets include:

- The Ghost of George Best
- The Golden Cup.

Their mission is to help Benji to get his anger under control (his swearing was dealt with by using strict communication rules in work-up sessions and role play).

The story begins with Benji waking up late and in a bad mood and getting angry with his mum. It escalates when he and Alex miss the school bus, and then again when he gets put out of registration for being rude. The big trial comes in football training when he is tackled by Alex. The *Homunculi* try all sorts of relaxation tricks but it is the ghost of George and his winner cup that saves the day.

CASE EXAMPLE 6: RYAN (SEE VIDEO CLIP 9 USING AN IPAD AND APPS)

Ryan is a highly intelligent boy with considerable observational skills and dramatic flair. He is also very artistic and enjoys the activity of drawing. Furthermore, Ryan was confident at navigating the iPad, Apps and accessing additional online resources. Ryan agreed to work on a creative project that might help other pupils with an angry attitude to teachers and other authority figures. Ryan's passions included skateboarding and playing his guitar. He created characters based on other children he met at his local skate park, and the character he admired the most became the *Head Homunculus*. Ryan enjoyed creating characters and talking about them, their superpowers and how they could help him. However, he found working with so many of them distracting. In the end, Ryan's story only used three *Homunculi* characters: The *Head Homunculus*, an Apprentice and Deficit Guy who is the mischievous miscreant. This character represented an impulsivity that is often the source of anger and inattention in teenagers. His gadgets included a flying skateboard and magical, electric guitar.

Having presented Ryan with the *Beano* sketch and the *Homunculi* films made by other children by way of an introduction, Ryan was keen to explore how he could create the characters and Skull backgrounds using the iPad and Apps. He decided to use the Puppet Pals 2 App which meant he could upload photos of his characters' drawings as well as images downloaded from the internet that approximated what areas inside the brain might look like. He also chose a set background from the App that featured windows similar to the eye department on the Skull poster. He wrote out thoughts, feelings and action speech bubbles to upload into Puppet Pals App scenes where the *Homunculi* communicate with the computer. The beauty of using the iPad and Apps like Puppet Pals is the capacity to create and upload your own characters (or create one from a drop down menu) into a background and to use 'drag' and record options to make the characters move and record what they say. There are also options for background music. In effect, the iPad and the App is a one stop shop for producing a complete, recordable movie which is saved to a shared or personal drive. It can also be saved and shared using a flash drive or DVD.

Ryan excelled at performance. He loved doing different voices and finding ways personally to act out the performances of all his characters. Whilst the first author played the voice role of an English teacher, Ryan played numerous roles: himself (before and after his *Homunculi* experience); Mr Cucumber the Head of English; and Mr Parsnip the Head Teacher. Ryan happily used materials lying around the therapy room as props. For example, he used tape and black paper to give his different characters defining beards, moustaches and eye brows. He was able independently to access his favourite guitar riff and add it to the cartoon. In the end Ryan produced a highly engaging and interesting movie, which can be viewed on the JKP Library.

Chapter 8

A Whole Class *Homunculi* Project - Primary to Secondary Transition

In recent times the primary–secondary school transition has developed into a complex 'rite de passage', with valedictory balls, proms and multiple school visits for all pupils in transition. Perhaps this can partly be explained by the ever present influence of trends in the USA and the Harry Potter sorting hat! All of this is, of course, fun and exciting. On the flip side there are the many typical worries that transitioning pupils have about going to high school. These include such things as: making new friends, being overwhelmed by too much homework, not being able to do the work in the first place, bullies and peer pressure.

Feeling nervous or excited about starting secondary school is both common and normal. Indeed most children manage the move to secondary school without any real difficulties. Some children, however, are vulnerable during the primary to secondary transition, and if they are not sufficiently supported throughout the process they can experience poorer immediate and longer-term outcomes compared with their peers (see White, 2020, for a detailed review).

Local Education Authorities in the UK do recognise the needs of all their pupils during the primary–secondary transition phase. To this effect they have programmes for preparing all children at the end of primary school – in Scotland this is Primary 7 – as well as individualised programmes (largely implemented through Child Planning Forums set up by education authorities) for those at risk. Typically, this involves high school staff visiting pupils in Primary 7 so that the teachers and pupils can get to know each other and have their questions and anxieties addressed. There are visits for all Primary 7 pupils to the high school over a two-day period, usually in the June of the year of transition.

In addition there are systems in place for identifying those vulnerable pupils who will require extra monitoring including additional assisted high school visits, auditing of specific classes or subjects and participation in high school activities.

However, at the time of writing, there is no known targeted, whole class approach to transition planning that focuses on specific worries about the process: the thoughts, feelings and actions involved, as well as how to manage the specific social situations that worry the pupils most of all.

The earlier chapters of this edition of *The Homunculi Approach* focus on using the technique with individual children or targeted groups of children. In Chapter 2 we reported on some new data we obtained in our ongoing *Homunculi* research: the results of an intensive case study of one school using *The Homunculi* for an entire Primary 7 class in preparation for transition to high school.

In this chapter we further explore the nuts and bolts of using *The Homunculi* to support all children going through the primary to secondary transition phase. In the particular example we describe here, the class included pupils with additional support needs. This allowed us to explore not only the general benefits of *The Homunculi Approach* to transition, but also the particular benefits for the most vulnerable participants who are included alongside their peers.

ORIGINS OF THE *HOMUNCULI* PRIMARY-SECONDARY TRANSITION PROJECT

A few years ago, early in the new school session, a creative and innovative headteacher, Mrs Davis, approached the first author about Primary 7 pupils with additional support needs as she had some concerns about a successful transition to the local high school. This was a sufficient source of concern to her that she wanted to explore alternative forms of secondary school education as well as other strategies that might be implemented over the course of the year to improve their outcomes for transition and beyond. Mrs Davis was familiar with the use of *The Homunculi Approach* with targeted individuals, pairs and small groups of pupils, so there was a discussion about the possibility of a project in which these vulnerable pupils would receive an intensive individual *Homunculi* programme, followed by a joint programme, with both programmes focusing on transition themes. After some further discussion around this, Mrs Davis asked: 'Do you think we could just do *The Homunculi Approach* to transition with the whole class? These pupils have all grown up together and in some ways there has been a mutual impact on all of them. I think they would all benefit from it and enjoy the activities.'

At this time within the field of educational psychology there has been a big impetus for a greater use of 'universal' approaches to interventions in education settings. This means the application of interventions at a whole class, whole school or indeed whole local authority level. It was an intriguing and entirely appropriate proposition by an experienced headteacher who wanted to make sure that *all* her pupils were included and supported. Such a project on this scale would further obtain best value for the largest number of pupils.

There is no other known universal, whole class approach to transition planning around the specific worries of children about the process. We believe there is also no other approach which could be as engaging, exciting, fun and educational and which has clear links across other areas of the curriculum. In addition, the approach would help to give the young participants a greater sense of autonomy and mastery of their own learning, dealing with their own worries using social problem solving and working with the help of their peers to come up with solutions.

As very many people using this book will be frontline practitioner teachers or support staff in education or care settings, we asked Kiersty Travers, an expert teacher who has often used *The Homunculi* at an individual, pair, group and class level, to give us her unique expert teacher view on how to implement *The Homunculi* at a whole class level around the theme of transition.

PRIMARY SCHOOL *HOMUNCULI* PROJECT - A TEACHER'S PERSPECTIVE

First of all, Ms Travers described what the standard primary–secondary transition plans were for all schools in her locality.

> During the final term (April–June) all of the Primary 7 classes in the local cluster complete a transition project that was devised by the local secondary school some time ago. The children complete a number of written tasks that are collated into a folder which they then take with them to secondary school. Their new teachers can look at the folders to help them get to know the children quickly and to get a good idea of the usual standard of written work. Staff from the secondary school also visit each of the primary feeder schools during the transition project. Depending on staffing, they try to arrange a visit from various members of the secondary school team. These include: a member of the Guidance team, a teacher from the Pupil Support team, a group of senior pupils and a visit from the Junior School Deputy with two former pupils who are currently in S1 (first year of secondary school). The children always find the visits useful and reassuring. There are two Induction Days in June where all of the Primary 7 pupils in the cluster attend the secondary school and meet their new classmates and teachers.

Whilst Ms Travers considers this to be a good programme that generally works well for most children, she felt that those children who took part in the *Homunculi* Primary–Secondary project had a greater advantage:

> I have taught Primary 7 for seven years (each time with the same prescribed transition project as described above) and I can honestly say that this class were the most prepared and most confident cohort of children I have ever helped through transition to secondary school.

She went on to explain not only what she did with her Primary 7 pupils, but also how they did it together.

WHAT MS TRAVERS DID

In initial discussions with Ms Travers, the headteacher and the educational psychologist, it was considered how flexible the programme could be in terms of delivery. It could be done once a week over the course of a term, or as an intensive block over a week or two, in much the same way as might be considered for individual or other group programmes. This was an important consideration because it was necessary not to overlap with the standard transition plans, whilst also making sure other teaching targets were delivered. Other considerations, such as access to spaces for the breakaway groups and other visiting professionals, were also taken into account.

It was agreed that an intensive programme every day for a week would work best for Ms Travers's particular class of children. This week would include two days during which structured lessons on PowerPoint would be delivered by visiting high school specialist subject teachers. It was thought that this would bring an additional opportunity for the children to meet new teaching staff in advance of the transition and vice versa. To this end Ms Travers approached each of the high school subject departments and asked for teacher volunteers to come to the class at the start of the *Homunculi* week to deliver their relevant lessons. These lessons could, of course, be delivered by the Primary 7 teachers, but it was felt really important to include the high school teaching teams if possible.

There are several structured lessons on PowerPoint as well as their lesson plans in the photocopiable Resource Bank section which are also available to download from the JKP Library as an editable presentation and a complete PDF pack for each lesson. The *Homunculi* Project start-up lessons are entitled as follows:

> **Lesson** (optional): Technology – using tablets to create films, cartoons and using special effects
>
> **Introduction to *The Homunculi*** (required): Introduction – What are *The Homunculi* and how do they help us with problems? Plus a simple questionnaire (Socratic Questioning) to find out which children had specific worries so they can be put together in a themed film production team
>
> **Lesson 1a and 1b:** Health and wellbeing – Thinking skills

Lesson 2: Drama – Performance and film techniques

Lesson 3: Art – Creating characters

Lesson 4: English – Storyboard and script writing.

It should be noted that although the programme would normally recommend teaching on using the tablets, Ms Travers felt her class was already quite expert on that. She decided that she could move on to the *Homunculi*-specific lessons and complete the whole schedule within one week. The level of competency of the class in terms of using iPad and computers is a consideration and extra time may need to be built in for this.

Regarding the week that was reserved exclusively for *The Homunculi* Ms Travers noted: 'It was a very busy and at times hectic week, but the children responded well to having tight deadlines.'

In the next section, we learn how Ms Travers organised the week into each of the essential teaching and practical elements.

PROJECT OVERVIEW

Monday and Tuesday: All scheduled lessons as outlined above were delivered

Children were put into appropriate groups depending on their questionnaire results from the Introductory Lesson. (The questionnaire asked children to rate, on a scale of 1–5, a number of high school social scenarios in terms of 'How anxious do you feel about this?' An example would be a picture showing a pupil being alone in the lunch hall.) The questionnaire was conducted as part of a pilot study but it is not necessary for other participating classes to complete. Teachers can easily choose specific scenarios and groupings to suit the needs of their own class (please see the Resource Bank for examples of such questionnaires or quizzes).

The groups were called 'Production Teams' and the children very much enjoyed the activities of coming up with a name and creating a logo to represent themselves. The children produced some wonderful examples:

- Doodle Studios
- Word on Words
- Film Planet
- Pencil on Paper Studios (POPS)
- Team Too Tricky.

Each Production Team was given a typical 'going to high school' anxiety or problem to discuss (as they arose in their questionnaires and through whole class brainstorming) and each group would then be asked to focus on a particular topic. If a number of pupils were worried about bullying, they were included in the group focusing on bullying.

The problem scenarios the children generated included:

- Getting lost in the big high school
- Not being able to make new friends
- High school work being too hard
- Not coping with homework for so many subjects
- Being bullied/peer pressure.

Any work completed during the lessons could be used by the children in their final projects, but time was given on Wednesday for them to complete new and improved versions of their characters, storyboards and scripts.

Wednesday: Planning and creating

The class started the day by recapping everything they had learned over the previous two days. At this point the Production Teams already had some great ideas for their films, but Wednesday was the day for discussion and proper planning. Ms Travers made sure that she was available to help and support the Production Teams if needed, but she was also careful not to interfere or try to influence the children's plans.

Each team had to complete the following list by the end of the day:

- storyboard outline of the whole story
- script for real life characters (actors in role play)
- script for *Homunculi* characters (voice actors for cartoon characters, narrator)
- creation of *Homunculi* characters
- creation of inside the head setting
- creation props and special effects planning.

The class were given access to a wide variety of art materials such as paper, card, paint, pens and pencils. Each Production Team was given three iPads and a MacBook Air for the duration of the project so they had access to the internet and printer and were able easily to access their videos and animations whenever needed. Throughout the day Ms Travers made sure that there were opportunities for the Production Teams to share their progress and ideas with each other. She noted that this was a really useful teaching strategy as the children often made helpful critical comments and offered excellent alternative solutions.

Thursday: Filming

As all groups were filming on the same day, the Production Teams were fairly restricted by the spaces available around the school, but it was important that each group had their own quiet space with no distractions. There were only two adults working with the class, so it was not possible to give direct supervision to every group all of the time. The Production Teams had been coached on the rules of good group work during the introduction to *The Homunculi* and reminded that they were expected to behave themselves and stay on task at all times. They were so involved in the project that they did! They were told that the two adults would circulate between the groups to offer help and advice if needed.

Each group were given their three iPads with Puppet Pals (a free App which is a helpful tool for creating cartoon characters and settings/locations), iMovie and Camera installed. You can use any tablets or computers with a camera and basic video editing capability. There are also lots of other editing programmes available to suit whatever devices a school or unit uses.

The *Homunculi* part was 'filmed' inside the character's head using the Puppet Pals App. This part was completed fairly quickly: the children didn't feel self-conscious as they weren't physically appearing on screen. The scenarios took a bit longer to film as the children were more concerned about how they looked and didn't like making mistakes. However, they did enjoy watching all of the outtakes at the end of the day!

Friday: Editing

Each Production Team used iMovie on their MacBook Air to edit the films. Ms Travers subsequently completed the project with a class who used the iMovie App on the iPad instead and she reported that it was very quick and intuitive for the children to use.

Ms Travers's strategy of making time for the children to share their progress throughout the day enabled the rest of the class to provide feedback in a timely manner and ensured the Production Teams had time to respond to it. Time was given to re-film scenes or add new parts if needed as this would ensure that the films made sense.

You may find that digital native students do not require the formal Digital Technology lesson. For teachers who are unfamiliar with the technologies being used, a quick Google search will uncover lots of 'how to' videos. Information about the computer or tablet can usually also be found on the relevant operating systems' website.

CELEBRATING SUCCESS/REINFORCING LEARNING

One of the joys of doing a 'media' style project is the inherent opportunities to share the work produced and to celebrate the hard work and success by way of a big (or little if preferred) Oscar type awards ceremony.

Some classes who have done this also built in time at the very end to have a film premiere with just the Primary 7 pupils so that they could share initial comments about each other's work. In one case the educational psychologist (but it could easily be the principal or deputy head of the high school or even the primary headteacher) was invited to the class premiere to provide initial feedback about their marvellous movie creations. When the first author did this, what was striking about it was not just the fun and motivational element for the children as they giggled watching themselves and each other in the final films whilst munching on hotdogs and ice-cream, but just how interested they were in the learning elements of each production. It was a fantastic opportunity for wider discussions around the solutions to the typical worries that children have about starting high school. There was a great discussion about the many ways to solve such problems or worries as well as seeing each other as a source of help and understanding.

The red carpet 'Oscar' Awards Ceremony was a wonderful way for the class to celebrate the *Homunculi* Project and share their learning with parents and specially invited guests (VIPs), some from the local high school. The event was planned for mid-week of the last week of term so it could also serve as a booster session just on the brink of the long eight-week summer break before the actual start of high school in mid-August.

The plans were *big*! The pupils had been prepared for this event at the start of the project and knew it would involve a dress code, nominations, awards and speeches. A local celebrity would be opening golden envelopes (the first author's niece, an actress who has often appeared on television, agreed to take part) and announcing the winners of the various categories: best acting, best scripting, best film and so on.

A local hotel allowed the school to use the function suite and the wedding red carpet for the evening. The hotel staff even decorated the room for added effect, including two lifesize cardboard cut-outs of Hollywood stars Brad Pitt and Angelina Jolie, a photo opportunity corner, cafeteria style tables for the Production Teams (logos displayed on plinths at each table) and mocktails, juice and crisps at the children's tables. Parents sat in rows of chairs toward the rear of the room so that they could see the children receive their awards. Staff, pupils and parents dressed up for the occasion, which made it feel like a really special evening. Each film was showcased and the children talked about different aspects of the project. The school sourced small Oscar statues online and bought one for every pupil. In addition, each Production Team was presented with a different 'voucher' award. The overall cost was minimal and the evening was a huge success.

A summary of the films produced by Ms Travers's class is outlined below and can be viewed on the JKP Library:

- Doodle Studios worked on the theme of bullying. The main character, Emma, tries to make a new friend on her first day at high school. However, very soon, they are both harassed by the school bully. Emma's *Homunculi* work hard to help her calm down by posting suggestions to her and winding back time to reflect on how to change things. Meanwhile the friendship grows between the girls as they support each other against the bully and grow more confident. They decide to ignore him and stick together. The film ends with the pupils giving viewers tips for dealing with bullies.

- Word on Words Productions worked on the theme of being scared of getting lost at the high school when moving between classes. The main protagonist is Nicol (who has *Homunculi* characters such as Builder Bill the Fixer, Lucy Lu the Helper, Coach Shooter and Smarty Pie the unicorn who is a navigator). Nicol gets completely lost moving around school. The *Homunculi* explore the thoughts and feelings chart and use their superpowers – scoring goals to make Nicol happy; using magical glasses to hallucinate him into feeling confident; using a necklace that transmits good ideas to his head; using a welding tool to turn bad thoughts to good ones; and using the character Pie to help him navigate to classes. The red light system shows the problem is getting worse. Lucy Lu gives them all instructions to unfreeze Nicol. The film shows Nicol wandering around the school corridors and grounds, getting lost. The *Homunculi* enforce their powers, the alarm lights change to amber and Smarty Pie navigates him towards a teacher. Nicol responds and the alarm turns to green. The movie ends with the actors giving the viewers tips for those who are anxious about getting lost. The team included amusing outtakes and a time lapse of them working on bringing the project together.
- Film Planet worked on the theme of too much Horrible Homework. Luke passes out when he is given his homework. Meanwhile inside his head the *Homunculi* alarm goes off. The *Homunculi* present themselves and ask how they can help. Helpful Henry has a hammer that makes all your worries go away when he hits you with it; Brainiac Brian can read Luke's mind and find out what the problem is; Coach Cathy has a horn that makes everyone work twice as fast and a box of chocolates that makes Luke happy; Miss Sugar gives a sugar boost to make Luke feel better when he feels tired and unhappy; Bad Thought Bill likes to make Luke feel bad, but Worry Stop has magnetism to draw all the worries together and put them into the Worry Jail. The *Homunculi* check the Thoughts and Feelings Screen and see how worried Luke is. Miss Sugar gives him a boost but it does not work, so Brainiac delves deeper – the anxiety and worries are still there because Luke feels under pressure. Helpful Henry suggests that Luke spreads his homework over a few days. Outside the head, Luke's classmate has to throw water on him to revive him from his faint. He talks about his worries to his classmate about feeling unable to do all the work and the awful things that will happen if he doesn't do it, and also that he'd rather watch TV. Bad Thought Bill revels in Luke's distress. The *Homunculi* coordinate their efforts and get all Luke's worries into the Worry Jail. The film reports how Luke overcame the burden of the homework. There is an excellent stop motion go demonstration of the characters working as well as outtakes.
- Pencil on Paper Studios (POPS) worked on the theme of making new friends. Alex cannot find a new friend. No matter what she tries, nobody seems to be interested. The *Homunculi* set to work. Kylie has a magic tennis racket and scores a cheering hit but Alex is still upset after school and at night. She begins to feel that she does

not want to go to school and that nobody likes her – she thinks she is lame and feels left out. Jumping Jim, Thunderstorm, Kylie, Pops Man and Pops O'Matic set to work. They use Jumping Jim's hammer and Pops O'Matic's superpower popcorn to make Alex feel better and more confident. She approaches potential friends with much more confidence and exchanges phone numbers. The *Homunculi* have a party to celebrate. The film ends with outtakes and time-lapse project work.

- Team Too Tricky worked on a similar theme of the work being too hard (rather than too much). The lead protagonist Daniel faints and the *Homunculi* alarm is triggered. The Head *Homunculi* (King Daniel) summons them: Hannah Banana, Coach Sunny, Fix It Fred and Dylan the Apprentice. The Thoughts and Feelings Screen reveals that Daniel is overwhelmed by worries and is finding the work in Maths just too hard. Hannah Banana and Coach Sunny stay behind to work on the problem. Hannah Banana suggests peeling the problem back. Coach Sunny decides to brighten up Daniel's day with his magic sunshine wand. The following day Daniel has done some practice in his Maths but immediately needs to get help from the teacher. He listens carefully, then speeds through his work. However, he still gets a few wrong and the teacher tells him more practice is needed. The Head *Homunculi* uses his wand to make Daniel feel calm and Fix It Fred sets about tightening up some screws to keep Daniel on his homework tasks. The next day Daniel is very enthusiastic and positive, having practised all of the night before. He finishes very quickly and gets everything right. He is very happy. The *Homunculi* recap what they have learned and set up a party. The film ends with a time-lapse of working on the project.

Chapter 9

Frequently Asked Questions

Q: What if it is difficult to keep my participant focused or if he/she keeps coming back to an obsessive theme or idea?

A: This is most likely to happen with children who are autistic, have difficulties associated with a developmental difficulty such as moderate learning difficulties or ADHD, or the general planning, memory and organisational problems often seen as part of dyslexia or dyspraxia. Children with emotional and social difficulties can also be affected if they seek to control the agenda or have a coercive interactive style. In all circumstances, the scripted and rule-based nature of the programme is helpful, and indeed was designed with such difficulties in mind. If the participant wants to pursue his/her own inappropriate agenda or idea, remind them that in this activity the rule is to do whatever is appropriate to the development of the story next. It is quite simple and, if put across in a low-key, matter-of-fact way, it avoids debates and discussions that will not be fruitful in terms of story development. It therefore helps to revisit the rules of the game, which the participants learned at the start, when this sort of tension arises. Children with a diagnosis will require to refocus more than other children and you should allow more time for completion of the programme in such cases.

You can watch Video Clip 6 of Anne, one of the co-authors, working with two autistic boys as they are encouraged to follow an agenda, practise role play and create characters. You will be able to observe how she keeps them focused and on topic using repetition, using planned structured materials and bringing the boys back to the focus of the task in repeating the agenda, sticking to the agenda, a lot of repetition in role play as well as pointed questions during the creation of the characters.

Q: How do I encourage parents/carers to engage in *The Homunculi Approach* and help them to understand the benefits of it?

A: As a general rule, it is essential in almost all cases to ensure that the participant's parents or carers understand what *The Homunculi Approach* is and to obtain their informed consent for their child to engage with you. There are examples for parent and pupil information sheets available in the Resource Bank as well as downloadable templates on the JKP Library. These are exemplars that you can use as a template and customise for your particular setting and situation. An online introductory webinar is also available and it is important to check the content of that to ensure that it will meet the parent's needs in an appropriate way.

If you are working with an individual child therapeutically, the decision as to whether or not to involve the participant's parent/s should be made on a case-by-case basis. A boy in his mid-teens may not want to share his *Homunculi* experience with his parents and is old enough to give his own personal informed consent. This is rare, however, and even in the teenage years it is good to share products of the session with parents. This can be a good way to give parents an insight into their child's perceived problems and how they plan to solve it. The parents can then support their child by using what they have learned from the child's project when a situation arises again outside of the therapy or project room, for example 'Oh what would your magical goal keeper do in this situation?' In some cases parents have taken part to encourage their child into the process and to play parts.

With the explosion in digital technologies, it is now very easy to share the participant's products of *The Homunculi Approach* with parents. This can be done on an online shared drive, by email using facilities such as Dropbox and WeTransfer, or on concrete flash drives or DVDs.

Q: What should be done if a participant is obsessed by or being influenced by computer games or TV programmes involving violent and aggressive characters with guns and knives?

A: Set up a rule at the start that the *Homunculi* are a peace-loving species and gadgets cannot be guns or knives, and there should be no blood, death or destruction. Choosing a good metaphor (not about war) can help too. No doubt this will decrease the allure for some children, but the influence of multimedia in the wider culture is hard to avoid. For this reason, it is better to work non-judgementally with it and to try to turn a negative idea into a positive one. For example, if the participant suggests a gun with bullets that lodge in the brain and explode or a grenade to blow up enemies, you can remind them that it is not allowed in *The Homunculi* and look for the basic idea and an alternative type of gadget that would have a relevant positive impact. One participant suggested a calm-ray gun, but this was simply changed to a Calm Ray Device (rather than a gun) that emits positive energies by colour.

Q: What is the best way to manage *Homunculi* sessions involving more than one participant?

A: This really depends on the nature of the problem to be worked on and, to an extent, on the nature of the child. If the participant needs to do *The Homunculi* because of social difficulties, it is likely that at least one full programme should be completed alone before involving others. Others can be gradually introduced to the programme as the participant moves to new levels of skill. Those coming in to 'help' with a story will be recruited as that: a helper. Parental permission should be sought without betraying the difficulties of the participant involved. It could be helpful to say something along the lines of: 'I am working on a project with Tommy about how to help school children cope with bullying. We are going to make a film about it and he needs a friend to help with role play just now.' On the other hand, as in the case of one particular participant who had a social anxiety related to strangers and less familiar people (including the programme leader), it was necessary to bring her one little friend to help her cope.

Q: When working with a child or young person with learning difficulties, it can be difficult to get them to identify the characters with their actual problems. What is the best way to tackle this?

A: The secret to this is feeding the child the ideas initially. You will know what the issues are, so mention them. For example, use that reported 'playground incident' or that 'thing that happened in class' specifically. Invite them to talk a bit about it, then ask them what kind of agent might be useful to have around to help when this problem occurs. Make suggestions and let them choose if necessary (see further guidance in Boxes 5.1, 6.1, 6.2 and 6.3).

Q: Have the sessions failed if the pupil does not generalise what has been learned on the programme?

A: For the majority of pupils taking part because of typical reactive stress, depression, anxiety or anger, the learning should be effectively generalised. For pupils with neurological difficulties associated with ASD or ADHD, it is important to understand that the sessions are intended to support the child with difficulties and sometimes these difficulties cannot be overcome entirely, such as the sort described in Chapter 2. This means that generalisation is inherently difficult for some children. However, a well-designed and focused story plot that includes information from the participant, parents and school staff and targets specific issues should be highly effective in containing current problems, bringing scores down to sub-clinical levels and helping them through a current crisis. This does not mean the participant will not have future difficulties. In professional practice, it has been observed that children with neurodevelopmental difficulties will improve in their own targets for the specific problem worked on. This can be across contexts such as home and school if sufficient sharing takes place. However, the young participant could still experience a variant of the problem in accordance with developmental changes. For example, a child in primary school may obtain a good outcome on a project about being angry at others during the popular game known as Dodge-the-Ball and may never be angry again in that particular game. However, the rule may not have transferred to their behaviour in playing football. Another story around that will help that particular difficulty but will perhaps not stop them from developing an angry attitude at a later stage or secondary school when playing in football matches.

Q: What is advised when a participant has a very negative view of self, due to a diagnosis, or of other people and incorporates notionally 'inappropriate' elements in their story?

A: We, as authors, have both had direct experience of this. Being educational psychologists as well as psychotherapists, when a young person is referred to us for a service it is natural for them to be struggling to come to terms with news, changes and situations that are very challenging for them. The starting position for *The Homunculi Approach* programme leader is the same as it is for us: you have to begin with where the child is at. If the child is angry about a diagnosis, then it is essential to accept and understand this anger with them, whilst gently moving them towards a more adaptive view of themselves and/or others. This means you may have to work, creatively, for a time with exploding bombs whilst working towards alternative tools (e.g. gentle yet exciting/positive alternative suggestions such as a 'shrinking device').

Furthermore, with such vulnerable individual children, it is also recommended that other work is ongoing with the child, educators and parents on helping them to understand the child's diagnosis or challenging situation.

The approach will be different if you are working with a larger group or whole class of children. The preparatory work towards the creation of more functionally adapted tools should already have been done, in advance of the group work, with the more vulnerable children taking part.

Q: Some children are not good at writing or drawing or generally being creative, whilst some are shy and hard to engage. What is the advice for engaging them and is there any point if they just want to talk about characters?

A: *The Homunculi Approach* is designed to be flexible and relevant in all of these situations. Children as young as six have taken part and their skills across the board are quite different to those who are in their sixth year of high school. I, Tommy, have worked for many years with children with very significant disabilities and found that even just talking about the idea of the *Homunculi*, who they are and what they do, as well as helping them to create the characters, still resonated and helped children who have significant barriers to full-on engagement.

In the Nuts and Bolts chapter earlier in the book there is reference to the many online tools that can be used to enhance engagement with the reluctant or challenged participant. Images can be downloaded from the internet. Templates can be used, as well as the programme leader generally 'helping' or 'scribing for the child'. The secret to engaging the reluctant or challenged child is to work creatively with their passions and interests and at an appropriate level of difficulty according to ability. Teachers will be familiar with this concept as 'the spiral curriculum' and this is exactly what is required here.

Q: Can *The Homunculi Approach* be used with neurotypical peers to increase awareness, empathy and understanding of issues faced by some children?

A: The concept of neurodiversity has become quite a zeitgeist since *The Homunculi Approach* was first published in 2013. In part this is due to the rapid advancement of the trauma-related ACEs (Adverse Childhood Experiences) movement and also in part due to the generally improving social awareness of a range of relatively common neurodevelopmental disorders such as autism and ADHD.

Education authorities' policies on inclusion also mean that schools have become experienced in both greater numbers of children with a formal diagnosis as well as those children who have really significant difficulties due to the severity of their diagnostic status. Including neurodivergent children within the mainstream setting requires recognition of the significant (yet often subtle) difficulties faced by these children at a resource level and at an everyday practitioner level.

In addition the inclusion of one or more significantly affected children within a mainstream setting can have a massive impact on the other neurotypical children. Indeed, this was the concern, but also the opportunity presented to the first author and a primary school head teacher when the concept of the transitions project was developed as outlined in Chapter 8. Whilst the project focused on the themes of transitions for all pupils, the themes could easily be around 'neurodiversity', or indeed a wider range of individual differences in children to include things like autism, ADHD, dyslexia, asthma, and visual and hearing impairment. The whole class project could focus on deeper exploration of one type of difficulty such as autism. In this example each production team could focus on a feature of the disorder that makes school life a challenge. Alternatively, the whole class could focus on a different type of difficulty.

As with *The Homunculi Approach* for individuals, pairs or small groups, the focus or theme of the programme is flexible and can be tailored to the specific needs of those children taking part.

There are now very good, child-friendly cartoons and films about autism, ADHD, dyslexia and so on, available online. These could be used by *The Homunculi Approach* programme leaders during the five initial teaching sessions, or using an additional, bespoke teaching session. In considering this question, the very first videos created by Ian, Video Clips 1, 3, 7a and 7b, are particularly relevant. He specifically identified his Asperger's

Syndrome and divided his themes and characters around specific difficulties he personally experienced including bullying, leading to magical tools and solutions. It is just a short step from this to a similar story plot for ADHD or dyslexia, for example, that can operate at an individual or larger group/whole class level.

Q: What is the target age range? Has *The Homunculi Approach* ever been used with preschool or nursery aged children?

A: The eldest participants in *The Homunculi Approach* to date have been in their sixth year at secondary school, hence about 17 or 18 years of age. The approach could potentially work with even older people with certain types and levels of learning difficulties who attend a day care facility. The youngest child who successfully took part in *The Homunculi Approach* with us was an autistic boy aged six, who had a fear of swimming pools. He absolutely adored dinosaurs and his characters included dinosaurs that could go into water and some that could not. He created an 'outside the head' swimming pool from a large roll of blue frieze paper and his Head *Homunculi* communicated with the others using phones whilst they ventured 'outside the head' to the swimming pool. There was very little adaptation needed in this case, other than limiting the time of each session and working with less mature material and language.

Working with the youngest preschool or nursery age children is a potential area of further research and development for *The Homunculi Approach*. Intuitively, we already know how beloved the Mister Men series (rather than the Numskulls) is with this youngest age group, and together with a spiral curriculum which advocates the view that anything can be taught to any age group with adapted age-appropriate concepts there is absolutely no reason that *The Homunculi Approach* could not be adapted and successfully applied in the same flexible manner as it was used with the eldest participants who were in their sixth and final year of high school.

Q: Does the approach work longitudinally with check-ins after school age and into adulthood to assess the effectiveness and applicability when used in the 'real world'?

A: At the time of publication, the best evidence for a longitudinal impact is to be seen in Ian's story. The reader is directed to the evidence base outlined in Chapter 2 about Ian's three sources of evidence: his own mental health measures; his personal reflections; and the views of his teachers and of his parent. Qualitative evidence is also available by following the videos in which Ian takes part throughout his high school experience (see introductory video feedback, group feedback and three-year feedback videos – available on the JKP Library). These videos take us on the journey from Ian's first year of high school until his final year.

Whilst we do not currently have formalised evidence of the journey into adulthood, the first author is in touch via social media with three of the original five participants who, at the time of publication of the 2nd edition of *The Homunculi Approach*, have entered their thirties. Two have become fathers and are holding down jobs and one is living and working abroad. All three remember their experiences of *The Homunculi Approach* vividly and with affection and have become productive members of society who no longer feel the need to rely on their original diagnostic status. One of them has ambitions to use the approach in a disability advocacy role. Regarding the two other original participants who do not keep in touch, one is often seen locally in his job which he has successfully held since leaving school and the other has left the area.

For the participants who have kept in touch, it is evident that the original challenges have reappeared at times of significant life changes such as starting a new job, relationship or upon becoming a parent. However, the ability to adapt, to communicate about it and find ways of coping has been impressive.

Regarding the question about the longer-term outcomes, it is important to note that the aim of *The Homunculi Approach*, in the case of a participant with a formal diagnosis of some kind, has never been to cure the participant. Rather, it has been used as a tool for what is known as 'psycho-education' – an approach that aims to increase awareness and resilience, to a point that the person's stress does not escalate to an unmanageable and clinical level.

Q: Would *The Homunculi Approach* work with children with most additional support needs?

A: To date we have both personally used the programme with children who have a wide range of additional support needs that include autism, specific learning difficulties, mental health disorders such as anxiety, depression, stress, eating disorders, low self-esteem, phobias, problems getting along with others/making new friends, sleeping problems, exam stress, anger management, bullying, everyday worries, coping with change, children who are looked after by the local authority, understanding a diagnosis and general moderate learning difficulties. There are likely more examples within our separate practices too. There is a good evidence base in relation to autism and autism-like problems for pupils in mainstream settings, including mental health difficulties and our new research looking into using the programme universally to manage worries with a whole class project for transition to high school. We are aware that there are a number of theses that have been done using *The Homunculi Approach* and this type of evidence base is ongoing and gradually unfolding. As a general rule, if your potential young participant can follow the logic of the programme and enjoys thinking about the characters and tools (even if you need to help create them), it is entirely fine just to try it and see how far you can go with it. *The Homunculi Approach* has been carefully designed to allow maximum flexibility in how it is done and who with. When the very first episode was created, there was nothing at all available that was known to work for hard to engage young people on the autism spectrum. The design also took into account that it might not work for a number of reasons in any one case, and if that happened, it was just fine so long as the participant had fun. Furthermore, there should be no risk of harm even if there is no progress for the participant.

Q: What do the authors recommend in terms of further research for programme leaders?

A: As *The Homunculi Approach* has been designed as a flexible programme that can be used across settings, ages and a range of difficulties of various levels of challenge, the authors consider that there are endless opportunities for future research. Here are some of the things that programme leaders, educators, students and others have raised with us:

- Looking in some details at supporting general transitions for children and young people on the autism spectrum: within the home, within the class, across classes, across schools, leaving school and so on.
- The use of the programme for children and young people who have experienced trauma.
- Working with children and young people in specialist behaviour units.
- Ways of supporting children and young people in the care system.
- Research into the use of the approach with young adults in work and/or college environments.
- Wider use in addressing clinically significant problems with mental health difficulties as phobias, complex developmental trauma, obsessive thinking, eating disorders, problems with anger, depression, anxiety, self-esteem and so on, with larger groups of participants.
- The development of an App along the lines of Puppet Pals.
- Using the approach on an area-wide basis as a standard part of the primary to secondary transition programme for all children.
- Other universal approaches, such as part of exploring neurodiversity.
- Establishing a curriculum slot within the Health and Wellbeing curriculum modules in the school/college context.

Part 3

THE HOMUNCULI RESOURCE BANK

Carrying Out the Programme: Templates and Resources

SAMPLE CARTOON

The Homunculi Episode 1 cont...
③
We still have a problem for Ian, but MacKay e Moody found a strange mobile phone....
HELLO
Who is that?
Maybe it's help — let's try it...
OK
Er... Hello?
ASPIE CONTROL AT YOUR SERVICE
Meanwhile Chatterbox checks the thoughts e feelings...
THOUGHTS
They are all bullies!
FEELINGS
I hate everyone!
OH DEAR
CHATTERBOX SHOUTS TO HURRY THEN TAKES COVER WITH COUCH POTATO e GAFFA.... AND ASPIE PLAYS WITH A BOMB
EEK!
Look it's ASPIE!
To be continued

The Homunculi Episode 1 cont.
④
So, Ian's still upset, Aspie has escaped, e a gadget is missing...!
Aspie is not trained in Gadget handling — we MUST investigate
THINK
Thinking Time Buster
Oh no! He's messed up the Gadgets!
EEK! LOOK
TICK! TICK! TICK!
It's WIRED TO BLOW....
RUN
Guys — I can defuse it!
Meanwhile outside the Skull....
Ha, you're not worth it!
Hmm — wonder whats up!
MEAN BOMB
ASPIE SHAKES IT
Kaboom
THOUGHTS
I'm in control
FEELINGS
It feels good
HURRAY
GO
THE END

BLANK CARTOON TEMPLATE

The Homunculi Episode

SOCRATIC QUESTIONING

- What do you know about this problem?

  ....

- Would your thoughts be accepted by others as correct?

  ....

- How can you find out whether or not your thoughts are correct?

  ....

- Are there other interpretations that fit the facts just as well?

  ....

- How might a friend of yours feel or think in the same situation?

  ....

- If facts are gloomy, does it help you to think this way?

  ....

- How does this type of thinking affect you?

  ....

- Does your behaviour make it worse?

  ....

- Do these thoughts help or hinder you in achieving your goal?

  ....

- Are you worrying about things you can't change?

  ....

- When you are not feeling this way, do you think about the problem differently?

  ....

- Is the problem really as bad as you seem to think it is?

  ....

- Are you over-reacting to small problems?

  ....

- Are you blaming yourself for things you can't control?

  ....

- Are you imagining the worst possible outcome?

  ....

- Are you jumping to conclusions without evidence?

  ....

- Are you thinking in extremes, black and white?

  ....

- Are you attaching too much importance to the problem?

  ....

MISSION SOLUTIONS

Mission: (e.g. to deal with being bullied and teased)

....

....

What I could do...	Good outcome...	Bad outcome...
e.g. Hit them OR	Makes me feel good	I get into trouble, suspended and they hit me back ....
e.g. Find an adult OR	Adult sorts it out and it stops	Maybe can't find an adult and the bullying gets worse ....
e.g. Ignore them OR	If I don't react they will get bored and give up	They may try harder and I get hurt ....
e.g. Stay away from them at the breaks OR	They can't tease me, I don't get into trouble or hurt and they do other things	They might try to find me ....

Solution: (e.g. On balance, it seems best to solve the mission problem by keeping away from them at break times and to tell an adult.)

....

....

AGENT AND MISSION

My name is Agent: ....

This is how I look:

It is my mission to: ....

....

....

....

THE GADGET STORE

My special gadget is: ....

This is how I look:

It works by: ....

....

....

....

MY STORY RECORD: BEGINNING

In the beginning:

He has been pushed into a fence

MY STORY RECORD: MIDDLE

Thinking time

In the middle:

....

....

....

....

....

....

....

....

....

....

....

....

....

....

....

....

MY STORY RECORD: END

In the end:

Hurray, let's celebrate

HOMUNCULI TEMPLATE

My name is: ....

My job is to: ....

....

SKULL TEMPLATE

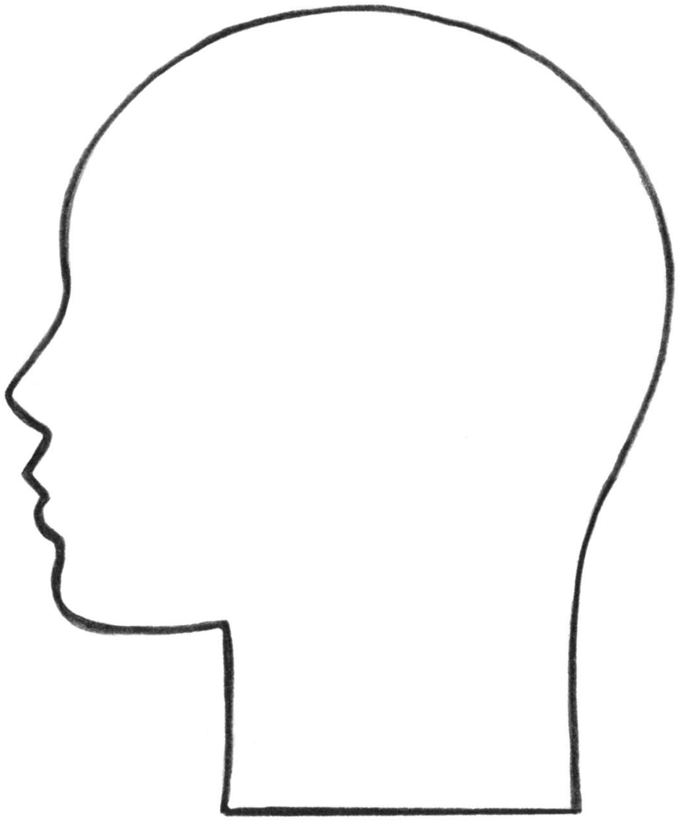

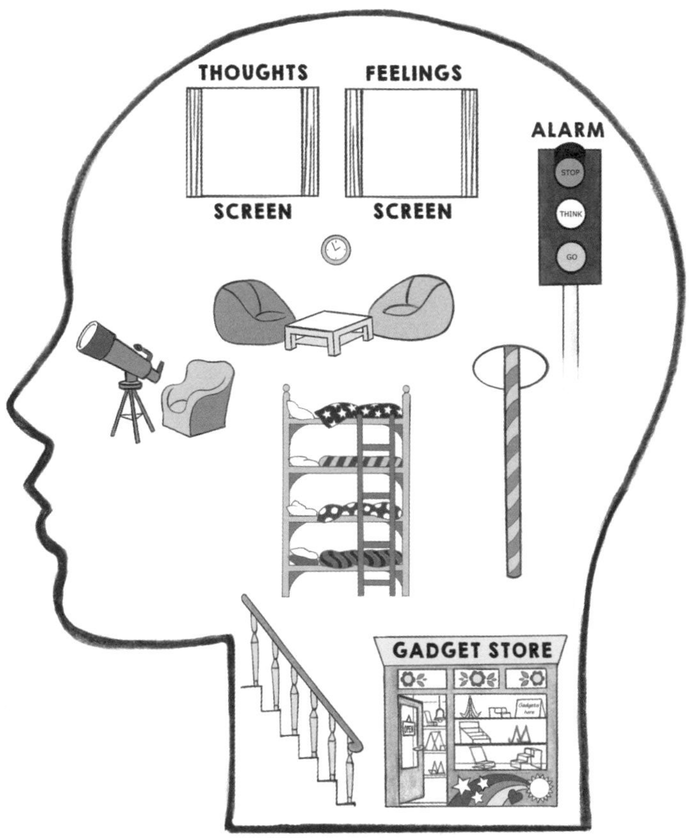

THOUGHTS AND FEELINGS SCREEN TEMPLATE

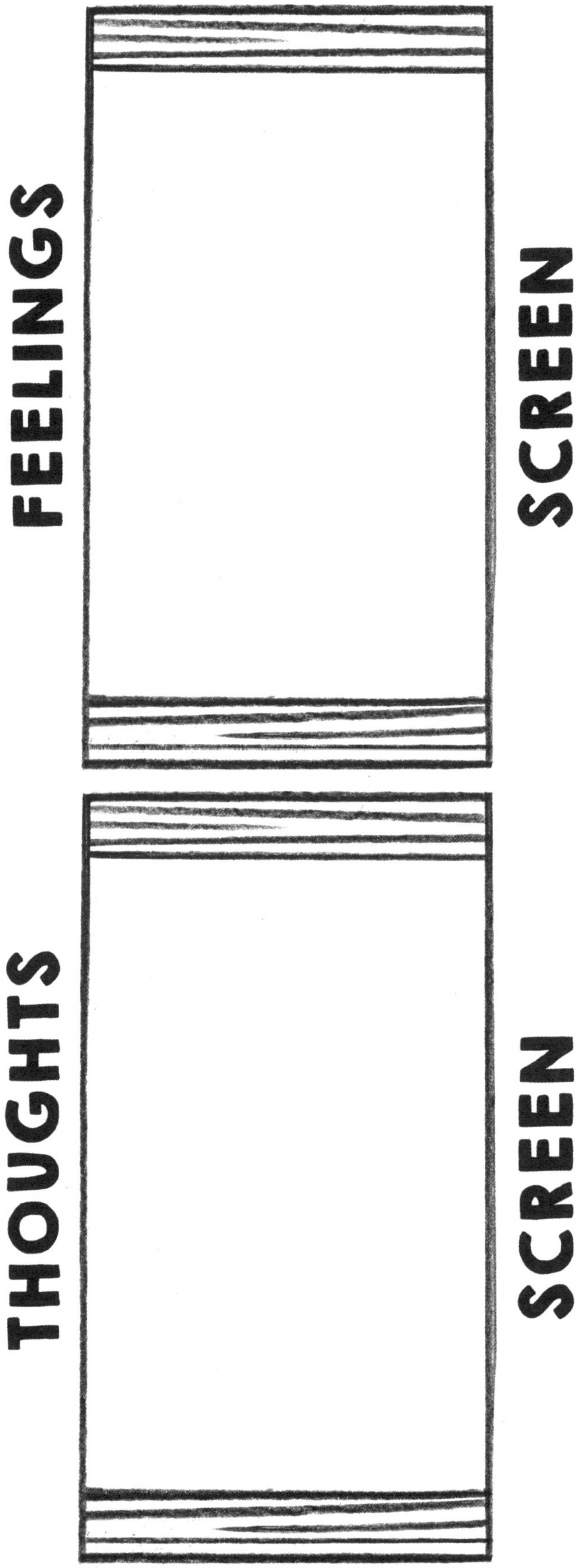

GADGET STORE TEMPLATE

TRAFFIC LIGHTS: STOP! THINK! DO!

ALARM

ARE YOUR *HOMUNCULI* WORKING FOR YOU?

BEFORE You Make Your Cartoon/Film

Can you plot on the scale how you feel you are coping with the problem of:

....

....

....

....

right now? Put a circle around the number:

Not very well ⟨ 1 2 3 4 5 6 7 8 9 10 ⟩ **Brilliant**

Now can you plot where you would like the *Homunculi* to help you to be? Put a X through the number.

AFTER You Make Your Cartoon/Film

Now that the *Homunculi* have tried to help you, can you plot on the scale how you feel you are coping with the problem of:

....

....

....

....

now? Put a circle around the number:

Not very well ⟨ 1 2 3 4 5 6 7 8 9 10 ⟩ **Brilliant**

Have the *Homunculi* helped you with this problem?

- No, it's worse
- It's about the same
- Yes, it's a bit better
- Yes, it's much better
- Brilliant, I can retire the *Homunculi*!

Whole Class Transition Project Resources

SCHOOL ADMINISTRATION DOCUMENTS: PERMISSION LETTERS (TO PARENTS)

X Primary School

Date....../....../......

X PRIMARY SEVEN – SECONDARY TRANSITION DIGITAL ARTS PROJECT

Dear Parent/Guardian

I am delighted to inform you that our Primary 7 pupils have the opportunity to take part in a joint project with our local high school to support them as they go into their transition to the secondary school programme.

This is an exciting project, which is scheduled to start on [date] and will involve the pupils in making cartoons and videos whilst at the same time learning how to solve every-day school related problems. The project not only aims to enhance the pupils' learning opportunities in art, storytelling, drama and filming, working with digital media and editing technology, it also aims to enhance their thinking skills when social challenges arise in the school context (e.g. bullying, exam stress, personal confidence, getting along with friends, difficult work, coping with homework, study and other pupils).

Your child will take part in five teaching sessions and follow-up workshops between (dates). The teaching sessions will be delivered by high school specialist teachers who have volunteered to take part in the project. The lessons include: thinking styles, art, story work, role play and working with digital media. In the follow-up workshops the pupils will break into small production teams [groups of ?], and each team will produce their own video. An awards ceremony, to which you will be invited, is planned for the X term [date]. An information leaflet on *The Homunculi Approach* is attached for further details. If you would like to talk to us in person about the project, please contact [name] who will answer all your questions.

The Homunculi Approach is already a successful publication for psychologists and school staff to use with individual children. As we plan to use the approach in a creative way, with an entire class of pupils, the authors and publishers may be interested in publishing examples of excellent work which your child may produce in collaboration with others. This could be a unique character or tool that is created, a clip of them in role play, or a video they have taken part in producing.

If you are happy for your child's work to be included in any forthcoming publications, I would be grateful if you could sign the permissions slip at the foot of this letter to indicate your preference.

If you do NOT wish your child to be involved in the project at all, please contact the school office on the above number as soon as possible, so that other in-school arrangements can be made for them while the project work is being undertaken in class.

I do hope that you will agree to your child taking part. Transition to secondary is an important step within the life of your child, and one that takes place more independently than other transition steps they have made in the past. As a nurturing school, we see real value in the teaching and learning associated with *The Homunculi Approach* and are confident it will have a very positive impact on each child as they prepare for their move.

Regards

[Name]

[Position], [School name]

- -

X PRIMARY SEVEN SECONDARY TRANSITION DIGITAL ARTS PROJECT

I/WE (NAME OF PARENTS)

....

GIVE OUR CONSENT THAT ANY WORK PRODUCED BY OUR CHILD [NAME OF CHILD]

....

IN COLLABORATION WITH OTHERS FOR THE *HOMUNCULI* PROJECT AT X PRIMARY CAN BE USED AS EXEMPLARS IN ANY PLANNED/FORTHCOMING PUBLICATION (JOURNAL, BOOK, KIT, ONLINE RESOURCE).

SIGNATURES OF PARENTS/GUARDIANS

....

Date....../....../......

Information for parents

Anne Greig and Tommy MacKay

Dr Anne Greig is a psychologist for Argyll and Bute Council, Scotland, and a practice tutor on the MSc in Educational Psychology at Strathclyde University. She has many years' experience as a teacher, researcher, applied psychologist and psychotherapist, specialising in mental health and the autism spectrum.

Professor Tommy MacKay is Director of Psychology Consultancy Services and Clinical Director of the National Diagnosis and Assessment Service for Autism Spectrum Disorders. He has over 50 years' experience working with children and young people with ASD and other difficulties. His work has won many national awards and has been described as making an 'outstanding and original contribution to psychology'.

The Homunculi (or 'little people') is a fun, cognitive behavioural therapy (CBT)-based activity that builds social and emotional resilience in children aged seven up to the teenage years. CBT is a technique used by psychologists to teach kids about the links between thoughts, feelings and behaviour and how to keep them balanced and in proportion. We initially developed the approach for kids on the autism spectrum who were finding school life challenging or those kids who were vulnerable for other reasons. Soon however we discovered that all kids, including those we do not normally see, not only enjoyed the programme but benefited from the strategies they explored in the process.

The story of *The Homunculi* began in our attempts to work with Ian (13). He refused to come to school and stayed at home with his hoody up. After a first difficult home visit, all we knew about Ian was that he liked computers and cartoons. During a coffee break Anne mentioned that she remembered a beloved cartoon from her childhood called 'The Numskulls' – a regular feature in the *Beano* comic, about these little guys that lived in a boy's head and who had an effect on the things the boy did, said, thought and felt. Basically, they lived in the boy's brain and were in charge of them, for better or worse! They also had cool gadgets like dream machines and snoring machines. Furthermore, there were departments within the boy's brain with special jobs: the ear department, mouth department and so on. As we reminisced on this, Tommy realised he happened to have a copy of the *Beano* in his briefcase and described how he had a Speedy Gonzalez character that appeared in his head when he has too much going on.

We went on to consider how this type of approach could be used with other kids like Ian, not only to engage them, but to provide them with a virtual executive function – what we psychologists call a metacognitive, or 'thinking about thinking', approach. The executive function is located in the front part of the brain. Its purpose is a bit like a pilot flying a plane or captain navigating a ship. That is, it is needed for monitoring, moving, focus, concentration, impulse control, planning, memory, organisation – all things that are known to be challenging for some children and young people as they develop.

We also spoke about the incidental similarities with the Mr Men series, and why, like the Numskulls, they caught the imagination of kids and became so popular. Out of this discussion, the concept of *The Homunculi Approach* was born. We could use these existing ideas to engage the children, then have them create their own 'little guys' who would have special jobs, tools and powers to help them with everyday problems. It would be rule based (must have a happy ending), scripted, have impulse control features built in (traffic lights) along with thoughts and feelings devices (emotion awareness training). In other words, the CBT would be built into the actual programme.

There is now really good evidence that kids benefit from scripted, social stories; visual approaches; the use of technology; rules and routines; and of course the love of cartoons and slapstick. So, we put it all together in one package: *The Homunculi Approach*. We then took the ideas back to Ian. He loved it. He had very definite ideas about what was hard for him: talking to people, making and keeping friends, nervous twitches, extreme emotions of anger and sadness and wanting to sleep all the time. He came up with his own ingenious characters to help him work out all the stuff that was so very hard for him every day.

More recently we have been using *The Homunculi Approach* with large groups and whole classes of pupils with the aid of iPads. This has the added advantage of being a one-stop shop with built-in filming potential and puppet drag technology where puppets can move and talk (you can take a picture and add your own face, whilst being recorded at the same time). We currently use a free download called Puppet Pals with older and more able kids.

In our School Project, we want to use the approach to help the whole class prepare for their approaching transition to secondary school by making films using *The Homunculi Approach*. In addition, because we have excellent technical expertise in [teacher name], every child will be able to work on and receive instruction on making films on the iPad. Teachers from the high school will take part in the project to teach the art of character and tool creation (Art Teacher), good story boarding (English Teacher) and good role play (Drama Teacher). The class will be divided into production teams (groups of X children) and we plan to have an 'Oscars' ceremony later in the session once the work is completed.

One of the most fascinating things in developing this programme was just how much insight kids have into the nature of their challenges and everyday worries when prompted to think about it. They are remarkably imaginative in the creation of characters and gadgets who they believe can help them to solve social problems.

Of course, it is always good practice to start with what interests the kids and to begin where they are at. Here is an example of an 'inside the head' metaphor of a group of teenage boys who were worried about the approaching exams.

The mission	Metaphor	Agents	Gadgets
To reduce stress associated with exams and distractions	The Brain is a Jungle	Data (elephant who never forgets) Lord Leo (lion in charge of Head) Kevin Bluewolf – a pack animal to deal with peer pressure DJ Radar to cope with noise in the ear department Blofelt – a weak character who blows up out of proportion, creates havoc and needs to be shrunk back down Aspie – a snake who gets up to mischief Jack Trainer – Aspie controller	A Proportionator and Aspie Detector to shrink Blofelt A sound deck and earphones for DJ Radar in the ear that neutralises sounds, turns down bad thoughts and turns up good thoughts

LESSON PLANS

For each lesson plan outlined below the wider range of support resources are available as follows:

- programme leader and professionals webinar
- downloadable Word versions of lesson plans
- downloadable PowerPoints
- downloadable support materials such as drawing templates, activity worksheets, quiz templates, administration documents such as information and consent letters
- downloadable PDFs of lesson plans and PowerPoints.

Please note that these lesson plans are based on the Scottish curriculum. The learning intentions and curriculum links can be mapped onto your local curriculum.

Preparatory lesson: An introduction to *The Homunculi Approach*

CURRICULUM LINKS

Curriculum codes given below are for teacher reference.

Through *The Homunculi Approach*, I understand that people have feelings and thoughts inside their mind and that people can behave differently in the same situation because of their different thoughts and feelings. I understand that it is important to talk about and manage these feelings. I am also learning how to work collaboratively with others. **HWB 0-01a – 4-08a**

Through *The Homunculi Approach*, I am becoming aware of how to express and manage these thoughts, feelings and actions through Drama: role play, movement, verbal and non-verbal expression, theatrical techniques and scripts. **EXA 2-15a**

Through *The Homunculi Approach*, I am learning how to express feelings and thoughts and the actions they cause through Art: the creation of problem-solving characters and tools. **EXA 2-05a**

Through *The Homunculi Approach*, I am learning the importance of writing techniques to make characters and plots interesting. **ENG 2-31a**

Learning Intentions	**1.** To be aware of the link between thoughts, feelings and behaviour in self and others as outlined in *The Homunculi Approach* **2.** To be aware that thoughts, feelings and behaviour can be managed and changed **3.** To be aware that it is possible to begin to understand more deeply the link between thoughts, feelings and behaviour using art, drama and storytelling, using technology and collaborating with others
Social Goals	**1.** To be aware that working alongside others can be fun and helpful when considering the different skills and creative talents they bring to a project **2.** To begin to consider what skills are needed for good team work
Success Criteria	**1.** Identify the kinds of worries pupils have about going to high school/ transitioning as well as personal worries **2.** Appreciation of how *The Homunculi Approach* is helpful in identifying the thoughts, feelings and behaviours that are part of the social problems or worries pupils have about going to high school/transitioning **3.** Identification of personal skills and ideas for characters, tools and plots that could be used in a collaborative *Homunculi Approach* project **4.** Appreciation of the qualities and skills others can bring to a film making project

<table>
<tr>
<td>Activities/ Methodology

***Key Questions in bold**</td>
<td>
Introduce the learning intentions.
Go through the Introduction to The Homunculi Approach PowerPoint. Have a complete episode of the Numskulls cartoon (Beano) in the class for pupils to consult at any point in the creative process.
In Slide 3 make links between the little men inside Ned's Head and what The Homunculi means in Latin. Point out how there are special departments and staff in there as well as cool tools like a dream machine and a snoring device. Why would it be really cool if we really did have little men like this inside our heads?
Explain that just as Ned's Numskulls help him with problems outside the head, The Homunculi can be personal to us and can help us with everyday problems. Do you think your little men or Homunculi would be the same or different to the Numskulls? Why?
Discuss the characters created by other pupils in Slide 4. Explain the two different approaches: a mixed metaphor (including Luke Pillow Walker) and the Jungle (with Jack Trainer). Can you think of other metaphors/themes that could work well?
Download and show:
<ol>
<li>Alex and Liam working on Nightmares and Getting along with other problems
Discuss the characters, themes and magical tools and the skills pupils need to make such a film. Do you think these boys worked well together? Why? What do you think of the characters and magical tools? Can you think of others they could have used?</li>
<li>Any one of the uploaded films on transition to high school
Discuss the worry, the characters, the magical tools and the solutions to the problem.
Discuss the characteristics that the pupils consider essential for a good Production Team with four or five members. Do you think these pupils worked well together? Note their answers down so they can be displayed on a flip chart or a frieze as an ongoing reminder to the pupils.</li>
</ol>
At Slide 6, mention there will be an awards ceremony with a local VIP (can be head of the new school or an actual celebrity if one is available and willing). Take the opportunity to reinforce collaborative working by pointing out that one of the awards will be for Best Production Team.
At Slide 7 there is an activity break with an opportunity to brainstorm what the pupils think will be worrying them about going to high school. It is also an opportunity to explore what they will be excited about. Now that we have looked at the sorts of things pupils your age worry about, what do you think might be challenging at high school? What sorts of things are you looking forward to and feel more confident about? A social situations quiz (please see examples in the book Resource Bank and downloadable resources at the JKP Library) can be used either before or after the brainstorm.
Slide 9 introduces the Production Teams. It is possible to assign the pupils based on their quiz responses to particular themes for a given team. However, group composition is also important, so this is at the teacher's discretion.
Slide 10. Brainstorm the names of some big production companies of movies the pupils may already know about. Show examples created by other pupils. If there is more than one good idea for the name of your team, is there a way to use all the best suggestions?
Slide 11. Create spaces for each Production Team to work together with art materials to brainstorm and agree on their own Production Team name and create a Logo which will stand on their work space as they work.
</td>
</tr>
</table>

Resources	Introduction to the *Homunculi* PowerPoint A3 sheets of paper or frieze paper and/or a flipchart and pens Art materials to create the Logo display Insertion of videos into the PowerPoint or links to the downloadable videos Laptop and projector Quiz/zes for each pupil (see Resource Bank/links) 1 hard copy of *The Beano* (with an episode of The Numskulls)

LESSON 1: THINKING SKILLS

CURRICULUM LINKS

I am aware of and able to express my feelings and I am developing the ability to talk about them. **HWB 0-01a – 4-01a**

I know that we all experience a variety of thoughts and emotions that affect how we feel and behave and I am learning ways of managing them. **HWB 0-02a – 4-02a**

I understand that my feelings and reactions can change depending upon what is happening within and around me. This helps me to understand my own behaviour and the way others behave. **HWB 0-04a – HWB 4-04a**

I understand the importance of mental wellbeing and that this can be fostered and strengthened through personal coping skills and positive relationships. I know that it is not always possible to enjoy good mental health and that if this happens there is support available. **HWB 0-06a – HWB 4-06a**

I am learning skills and strategies which will support me in challenging times, particularly in relation to change and loss. **HWB 0-07a – HWB 4-07a**

I understand that people can feel alone and can be misunderstood and left out by others. I am learning how to give appropriate support. **HWB 0-08a – HWB 4-08a**

<table>
<tr><td>Learning Intentions</td><td>1. Understand the link between thoughts, feelings and behaviour in self and others
2. Understand that thoughts, feelings and behaviour can be managed and changed</td></tr>
<tr><td>Social Goals</td><td>1. To develop social collaborative strategies and social problem-solving skills
2. To appreciate that thoughts, feelings and behaviour have an impact on fostering positive social relationships when well managed</td></tr>
<tr><td>Success Criteria</td><td>1. Identify different types of bad thoughts
2. Identify the relationship between thoughts, feelings and actions
3. Explain the STOP! THINK! DO! technique for controlling thoughts and actions</td></tr>
<tr><td>Activities/ Methodology

*Key Questions in bold</td><td>Introduce the learning intentions.
Work through Lesson 1 Part 1 PowerPoint looking at the different types of Bad Thoughts on the slides. Write each Bad Thought on a separate piece of A3 paper or page of your flipchart.
Bad Thoughts
Beating Yourself Up
Negativity
Fortune Telling
Catastrophising
Mind Reading
The Blame Game
Blowing Things Up
Snowballing
Dustbin Labelling
Heart Over Head
For each one, generate discussion. Ask the children: Can you think of examples of when this might happen? Write their ideas on the A3 paper or flipchart page to display in the classroom. It is really useful to refer back to these throughout the week.
Look at the five different ways to stop Bad Thoughts on the slides.
Dealing with Bad Thoughts
1. Notice it is there and label it.
2. Now leave it alone.
3. Stand up to it.
4. Be your own best friend and give yourself a break.
5. Think: what would a good friend say to you about such thoughts?
BREAK – take time out before starting the second part, otherwise it becomes too much for the children to think about at once.
Work through Lesson 1 Part 2 PowerPoint. Start by recapping on what was covered in the previous part of the lesson.
Ask the class How can Bad Thinking mess up your friendships? Look at the example of meeting Alex at a party. Emphasise that thoughts directly affect feelings and actions. Discuss each slide and highlight how feelings and actions change when the Bad Thinking changes to Smart Thinking.</td></tr>
</table>

<table>
<tr><td></td><td>Thoughts Affect Our Bodies. Show the class the big juicy lemon. Instruct them as follows: Close your eyes. Imagine holding this big juicy lemon in your hand. See yourself taking a big bite out of it. What do you think? What happens to your mouth? What do you do with your face? Cut the lemon in half, then take a big bite from it (if you are feeling brave) or pretend you are about to bite into it. You will see a physical response from most children. Discuss this THINK, FEEL, DO reaction.

Explain the Think–Feel–Do Circle. Jo gets told off for talking in class. Discuss her thoughts, feelings and actions in each example. What other thoughts, feelings and actions might Jo have had in this situation?

Look at the example of Tim and John. What is Tim thinking and feeling? Give the Production Teams five minutes to discuss the points on the slide. Groups then feed back their ideas to the class.

Group Discussion Points

1. Evidence for/against the rumour?
2. What would somebody who cared for Tim say?
3. What would you say to your best friend who has these thoughts?
4. Could Tim be having unhelpful bad thoughts? Which ones? Refer back to the notes on A3 paper from the earlier session.

Look at the different solutions suggested on the slide and discuss the possible good and bad outcomes. Can you think of anything else Tim could do?

Discuss Jo's thinking errors following an argument with her last friend. For each slide ask What does Jo feel and do?

More Thinking Errors

Catastrophising
Not noticing when good
Noticing only bad thoughts
Jumping to the worst conclusion
Ignoring good feedback about self

Explain that bad thinking leads to bad feelings and bad actions.

Introduce STOP! THINK! DO! which is based on traffic lights. Thoughts lead to feelings and feelings lead to actions. If the thoughts are bad, you act badly. But we can monitor our thoughts and try to stop them before we act. Using this technique we can develop our skills. Use the final slide to generate some discussion about different situations. This is the technique that our Homunculi will use to solve the problem in our scenarios. Display a large copy of the STOP! THINK! DO! traffic lights with the Thinking Errors in the classroom.</td></tr>
<tr><td>Resources</td><td>Lesson 1 Part 1 PowerPoint
15 A3 sheets of paper or a flipchart and pens
Lesson 1 Part 2 PowerPoint
Laptop and projector
Big juicy lemon and knife to cut lemon
Large copy of Traffic Lights STOP! THINK! DO!</td></tr>
</table>

Lesson 2: Drama, Performance and Film Techniques

CURRICULUM LINKS

I can create, adapt and sustain different roles, experimenting with movement, expression and voice and using theatre arts technology. **EXA 2-12a**

Inspired by a range of stimuli, I can express and communicate my ideas, thoughts and feelings through drama. **EXA 2-13a**

I have created and presented scripted or improvised drama, beginning to take account of audience and atmosphere. **EXA 2-14a**

I can respond to the experience of drama by discussing my thoughts and feelings. I can give and accept constructive comment on my own and others' work. **EXA 2-15a**

When I engage with others, I can respond in ways appropriate to my role, show that I value others' contributions and use these to build on thinking. **LIT 2-02a**

I can discuss and evaluate the structure, characterisation and/or setting using some supporting evidence. I can discuss the writer's/director's style and other features appropriate to the genre. **ENG 2-19a**

Learning Intentions	**1.** Compare different film techniques used to engage and influence the audience **2.** Create role play using our voices, facial expressions and movement
Social Goals	**1.** Work collaboratively with other members of your group **2.** Listen to and respect the ideas and opinions of others **3.** Share your ideas and opinions with others
Success Criteria	**1.** Identify examples of different camera shots and explain the effect they have on the audience **2.** Use voice, facial expressions and body language effectively to create realistic role play scenarios
Activities/ Methodology *** Key Questions in bold**	Introduce the learning intentions. Work through the Lesson 2 PowerPoint looking at the different film techniques on the slides: *Film Techniques* Low camera shot High camera shot Eye level shot Close-up shot Point of view shot

	Discuss each technique. **Can you think of examples of where you have seen each shot used or think of examples of where they could be used?** If the children are stuck for ideas, you could use a fairy tale to model answers. For example, in the story of the Three Little Pigs, you could use a low camera shot to look up to the Big Bad Wolf when he knocks at the door so that he looks extra scary. **How does each shot make the audience feel?** Watch the clip of The Story of Erica from *The Witches.** (This clip successfully builds a feeling of fear and dread which could possibly upset some children. Teachers should take the time to recall the story of Roald Dahl's book and explain the relevance of the clip. It may not be suitable for all children and the use of professional judgement is advised.) **What film techniques can you spot in the clip?** It might be useful to pause the clip at examples. **What effect do they have on the audience?** Discuss the drama and performance techniques on the next few slides. Model good and bad examples of each. Involve the children, e.g. My character is feeling very anxious. **How does my face look? How does my body look? What does my voice sound like? How do I react to others when I feel this way?** *Drama & Performance Techniques* Body language Facial expression Use of voice Voice projection Interaction with other characters Position in shot Practical part of the lesson – may require moving location to a larger area such as the school hall. Children should work in their Production Teams and need an iPad (or other recording device) per group to experiment with different camera shots. Explain that the class will be given a scenario related to starting secondary school. The groups will be given a couple of minutes to discuss the situation, then role play the scenario. **Can you think of how you can use one of the film techniques we've learned about to emphasise something to the audience?** For example, use a low camera shot to show the angry teacher shouting at the late child. Use the iPad to film the shot to share with the rest of the class. After approximately 10 minutes stop the class and ask for a group to show their role play to the class. Also get them to share their video footage and explain how and why they have used the specific camera shot. The rest of the class can give feedback and offer suggestions to help the group improve. Model a response, e.g. *I really like how Susan's facial expression and body language really showed how nervous she was. Next time make sure you are facing the camera when you speak so the audience don't miss anything.* Repeat this process for different scenarios. Ask the children to come up with a scenario for the class to role play. *Example Scenarios* Arriving late for a class and the teacher gets angry Getting lost at your new school Someone getting bullied School work is too hard Making new friends Accidently getting off the bus at the wrong stop

Resources	Lesson 2 PowerPoint Laptop and projector Access to the internet Large space, e.g. school hall for drama activities Tablet or other recording device for each group
Other	The first part of the lesson that refers to the PowerPoint slides might be best conducted in the classroom, before moving to a larger space for the practical drama activities.

**The Story of Erica from The Witches video to discuss film techniques: www.youtube.com/watch?v=oiC54FkzlHU*

Lesson 3: Art - Creating Characters

CURRICULUM LINKS

Through observing and recording from my experiences across the curriculum, I can create images and objects which show my awareness and recognition of detail. **EXA 2-04a**

Inspired by a range of stimuli, I can express and communicate my ideas, thoughts and feelings through activities within Art and Design. **EXA 2-05a**

When I engage with others, I can respond in ways appropriate to my role, show that I value others' contributions and use these to build on thinking. **LIT 2-02a**

Learning Intentions	**1.** Create a *Homunculi* Character Profile **2.** Create an articulated cartoon character
Social Goals	**1.** Work collaboratively with other members of your group **2.** Listen to and respect the ideas and opinions of others **3.** Share your ideas and opinions with others
Success Criteria	**1.** Complete a *Homunculi* Character Profile **2.** Design and create a special tool for your *Homunculi* **3.** Design and create a *Homunculi* Character with moving arms and legs **4.** Draw realistic facial expressions to bring your character to life

Activities/ Methodology *** Key Questions in bold**	Introduce the learning intentions. The children should work in their Production Teams for the duration of this lesson. Remind the children that *The Homunculi* live inside the main character's mind and they will work together to control the person's thoughts, feelings and actions. Work through the PowerPoint looking at the five different types of *Homunculi*: *The Homunculi Team* Head *Homunculi* The Coach The Apprentice The Helper The Fixer Each *Homunculi* character needs a special tool that they will use to help create a positive effect for the person. Look at the special tools examples. **What other special tools might the *Homunculi* use? What effect will they have on the person?** Create a list of the children's ideas on A3 paper for them to refer to later if needed. Look at the example character profiles. Generate discussion by asking questions such as **Why is that a good catchphrase for The Coach? Can you think of any others?** Create your *Homunculi*. Give each group a set of profile sheets. Production Teams should decide who is responsible for each *Homunculi* character. It is down to the individual to complete their own *Homunculi* Character Profiles so they can decide what to draw, catchphrase, special tool, etc. Give groups approximately 10 minutes to complete, then present to the rest of the class. **What do you like about this Team's ideas? What could they do to improve?** Bringing your *Homunculi* to life. Get the children to experiment with and demonstrate different facial expressions. **If I'm feeling frightened how will my face look? What will my facial expression look like if I'm excited?** Look at examples of how to draw different types of facial expressions using the link on the slide or address noted below. Follow the instructions on the slides to create articulated cartoon characters. Each child will need a sheet of white card, scissors, four split pins and a variety of pens and pencils. Give the children the opportunity to share their completed characters with the rest of the class. **What do you notice about how it moves? Will that work for your story? How can you improve it? What will you change? Is there anything you'll keep? How will that work on your chosen animation app?**
Resources	Lesson 3 PowerPoint Laptop and projector Access to the internet White card Coloured pens and pencils Split pins (four per child) Photocopies of Character Profile worksheets – one of each of the five characters for each Production Team A3 paper and pens
Other	Although most of the children didn't use the articulated cartoon character that they made in this lesson, it was useful in helping them consider how the *Homunculi* could move in the animation app. They made an improved version of their *Homunculi* on Wednesday.

How To Draw Facial Expressions step-by-step instructions: www.drawinghowtodraw.com/stepbystepdrawinglessons/2019/09/facial-expressions-and-silly-cartoon-faces-reference-sheet

Lesson 4: English - Storyboard and Script Writing

CURRICULUM LINKS

When I engage with others, I can respond in ways appropriate to my role, show that I value others' contributions and use these to build on thinking. **LIT 2-02a**

Having explored the elements which writers use in different genres, I can use what I learn to create stories, poems and plays with an interesting and appropriate structure and interesting characters and/or settings. **ENG 2-31a**

Learning Intentions	**1.** Plan a story using a storyboard **2.** Create a script for the story
Social Goals	**1.** Work collaboratively with other members of your group **2.** Listen to and respect the ideas and opinions of others **3.** Share your ideas and opinions with others
Success Criteria	**1.** Work collaboratively to plan the outline of the story using a storyboard **2.** List props and additional things needed for filming **3.** Use the conventions of script writing to create a script
Activities/ Methodology * **Key Questions in bold**	Introduce the learning intentions. The children should work in their Production Teams for the duration of this lesson. Explain that storyboards are used to plan films, TV programmes and animations. They show how the action should look on screen. Recap film techniques and how they can be used to influence the audience. Look at the slide with the example storyboard and list of props. Discuss the main features and how it is similar and different from a story. Remind the class that their story should show the problem, then cut to the *Homunculi* in the head who work together to STOP! THINK! DO! Then cut back to real life and have a resolution where the problem is fixed. Give each Production Team some blank storyboards and give them time to work together to come up with the main outline of their story and complete their storyboard. Display a large copy of the example storyboard on the wall and give each group a copy too. Refer to the storyboard checklist on the slide. If needed, you could work with the whole class to complete a large copy of the blank storyboard together to model the process. *Storyboard Checklist* Beginning, middle and end Outline of story only Note camera shots to use Sketch pictures – don't need to be perfect List props and things you will need

	Give the Production Teams the opportunity to share their work with the class and provide each other with feedback. **Does the story make sense? What works well? What could they improve?** Discuss the features of a script on the slide. Click the link or use the address below to look at example scripts that are suitable for children. Identify the key features. Ask questions such as **How are the character directions written? How can you tell the difference between directions and dialogue?** *Features of a Script* Description of the scene Dialogue for actors Character directions (within speech) Stage directions Special layout Look at the example script on the final slide. It would be useful to share a printed copy with each group and have a large copy on display for the class to refer to. Identify the key features of the script. Ask for volunteers to act it out. Look at the example script and example storyboard together and ensure the children see how they work together. Give the children time to write a first draft of their script. If possible, allocate each group a space where they can practise their script and make adjustments where necessary. If time allows, each group could perform their script to the rest of the class and provide feedback to each other.
Resources	Lesson 4 PowerPoint Laptop and projector Photocopies of blank storyboards Photocopy of example script and example storyboard for each group Large copy of example storyboard Large copy of example script Paper and pencils Lined paper
Other	The focus of this lesson should be the process of the Production Teams working together to solve the problem for their main character. Encourage the children to share ideas, listen to each other and work collaboratively to come to a shared agreement on the main events in their story and the outline of their scripts. They will have an opportunity to write a final draft of their storyboard and scripts on Wednesday, so the emphasis shouldn't be creating a polished final piece today.

Examples of scripts suitable for children: www.lazybeescripts.co.uk/YouthTheatre/NineToTwelve.aspx

INTRODUCTORY CLASS ACTIVITIES

In this section you will find samples of DIY Tools such as a Quiz/Questionnaire that can be used to stimulate class interest, brainstorm situations or for you (or your participants) to evaluate progress made from before and after the project.

ACTIVITY 1: HOW WELL DO I THINK I COPE NOW

Please rate where you think you are on a scale of 1–5 in each of the following scenarios.

- 1 is 'not coping at all'
- 2 is 'coping a bit'
- 3 is 'coping sometimes and not coping sometimes equally'
- 4 is 'coping a lot of the time'
- 5 is 'coping all the time'.

Please circle your number under each scene.

1. It's your first day at the new school. You do not know anyone there. When you go to lunch, you are on your own.

1 2 3 4 5

2. The Maths teacher at your new school describes a new problem. Everybody is working away but you did not understand any of it.

1 2 3 4 5

3. You have been at your new school for a week now. It is very big, and you keep getting lost. One day you are late for class and don't know where you are.

4. You promised your new friend you would go to the cinema to see the latest block-buster but have fallen behind on your homework.

5. You have six exams in a row at the new school. You have been hanging out with your friends instead of studying. You need the grades.

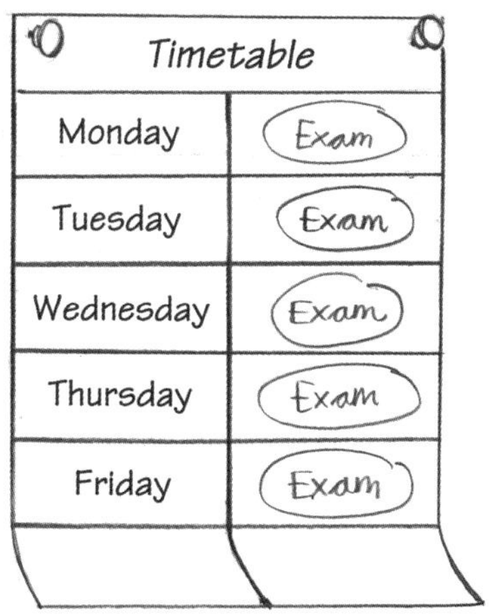

6. You have never liked speaking in public, but you have just found out that you need to do a speech for your class as part of the course.

1 2 3 4 5

7. You are with a crowd of friends when one of them pulls out some cigarettes. Some of the others light up. You want to say no but think they will laugh.

1 2 3 4 5

8. It's your second week at the new school and you still have not made any new friends. Everyone else seems to be in a group of their own.

1 2 3 4 5

9. You made a new friend who seems cool and funny. One day they tell you some of the others are planning to bunk school and wants you to come too.

1 2 3 4 5

10. A couple of older students at the new school have been saying mean things to you. One day they threaten you and take your money and packed lunch.

1 2 3 4 5

11. At the new school, a friend is having an all-night party. You don't want to feel left out by not going. Your parents say no because you are too young.

1 2 3 4 5

12. All of your new friends are chosen for a school sports team. You are not.

1 2 3 4 5

13. You don't like going on the school bus. The students can be annoying and rowdy and you can't 'walk away'.

1 2 3 4 5

14. You went to school wearing shoes that are not part of the school uniform. A teacher told you off. You got detention for saying, 'You can't tell me what to wear.'

1 2 3 4 5

15. One of your new teachers asks a question in class. You think you know the answer but feel too scared to put your hand up. You have been laughed at before for giving the wrong answer.

1 2 3 4 5

ACTIVITY 2: WHAT DO YOU THINK QUIZ

Answer each of the questions below by selecting the option that feels like what you are most likely to think in the given scenario by circling the letter next to the statement.

1. A class in one of your new subjects is tough. You don't think it's your best subject, so you are surprised to be in such a hard class. YOU THINK:
   - **a.** Oh no! There must have been a mistake. I'm no good at this subject. I'm going to mess up and don't know what to do. I'll be a total failure!
   - **b.** I know I'm not clever enough for this class but what can I do? I guess I should try but I'm not optimistic.
   - **c.** Well, I'm better at other subjects, so even if I fail in this class it's not all bad.
   - **d.** That's interesting! They must think I can do this work even if I don't think so. I will try my best and see what happens.
   - **e.** Don't know.

2. You are in a physical education class and you don't get picked to play in the team alongside your friend. YOU THINK:
   - **a.** I never get picked for the team. It's always the same when I really want something to happen. My friend is so much better than me. It's the story of my life.
   - **b.** Not again! How long is this going to happen to me? I must be better than my friend at something but I can't think of anything right now.
   - **c.** Oh well, I expected that, even if I hoped this time would be different. There's other things I can do better than my friend.
   - **d.** That makes sense. I know they will want the best players in a competition. It's not my best sport. I guess I just need to enjoy sitting out and doing my own thing. Yay!
   - **e.** Don't know.

3. You have a hobby that you really love and the school run a club for it after school. But you fell out with a student who already goes to the same club. YOU THINK:
   - **a.** There's no point in going. They hate me now and will have told everybody that I'm not nice and nobody will like me.
   - **b.** That's really annoying. If I go, it will be awkward. I'm not sure if I still want to go now. Probably not.

c. I don't see why I should miss out because they have fallen out with me. I suppose it will be annoying at first but I might get over it.

d. I will still go. It's about the hobby, not the people in the club, and it might be good for me to go. It's ok to fall out with people in the same club. I might meet new nice people.

e. Don't know.

4. It's the end of your first term at school and your report comes back with poor results. YOU THINK:

   a. Oh help! This is a nightmare! I've let myself down, I've let my teachers down, and I've let my parents down! I've let EVERYONE down. It's so bad. I'm never going to get to college or university now.

   b. Ouch! I knew it would be bad but this is really bad. People will be a bit disappointed in me. I'll have to work so hard to put this right now.

   c. Well, I expected that. I know I didn't study enough. I expect my parents won't be very pleased.

   d. That's what happens I guess when I leave it too late to study. Next term will be better. I will make a study plan and make sure all my work is done on time. I've learnt from this and I can tell my parents my plans to do better. They will understand.

   e. Don't know.

5. You have not been paying attention in class and the teacher asks you a question. You don't know what to say, so you just make something up. You get told off by your teacher. YOU THINK:

   a. Why do I always get caught? The teacher must watch me all the time to catch me out! I bet they don't like me much and now everyone will look at me and laugh.

   b. That is so unfair! I wasn't the only one not paying attention. In fact my friend was looking at their phone under the table distracting me. It was my friend's fault!

   c. We were all a bit distracted today. I guess the teacher just happened to look at me.

   d. Well, if you don't pay attention, this is what happens. Some other students got told off for not paying attention as well today.

   e. Don't know.

6. You are on a school sports team. You are the goalkeeper for the team. You get beaten 6–0. YOU THINK:

- **a.** It's all my fault. I let all those goals in. I let the team down.
- **b.** It's down to me. I'm having a bad day because I'm tired.
- **c.** Bad result, but I'm not the only one playing badly today. What were the other players doing?
- **d.** We all tried. The other team were better. Maybe I should have saved a couple of those goals but we were beaten by a better team.
- **e.** Don't know.

7. You are late for school and get told off in registration. Then you get told off for leaving your homework behind. Your friend is off, so you are on your own at lunch. In the afternoon you get an assignment back and it's a fail. YOU THINK:

- **a.** This is the worst day of my life. It just got worse and worse. What's even worse is that when I needed a friend to be there for me to talk to, they let me down too. What a disaster! And it's still only 3 o'clock.
- **b.** This has not been one of my better days. If only my friend had been there. There is a lot of homework to do as well.
- **c.** The only good part of today is going home.
- **d.** Well, I've had days that were a lot better than this one. Today is a one off. I can avoid this in future by not being late and leaving without my homework. I'll have a laugh with my friend tomorrow.
- **e.** Don't know.

8. It's your first lesson with Mr Meanie and someone you know told you that they are really strict and make you answer questions out loud in class, even if you don't know what to say. YOU THINK:

- **a.** Oh no! If they ask me, I'll freeze and everyone will stare at me and feel sorry for me for making a fool of myself. It will be awful. I will hate school on days where I have lessons with Mr Meanie.
- **b.** Aargh! I'm not going to like Mr Meanie's classes. I need to practise being invisible!
- **c.** Gosh! I'm going to have to pay a lot of attention in Mr Meanie's class. If I do, I might be ok.
- **d.** Well, what the person I know told me might not be true. It could be a nasty rumour. Most teachers I know are great. I'm not going to bother about this now. I'll wait and see and be sure to pay attention and try my best.

e. Don't know.

9. There's a cross country race and there are prizes for first, second and third place. Your three best friends all win a prize. You are one of the last to finish. YOU THINK:

   a. I am such a rubbish runner. When it comes to running I'm always the loser. I wanted to be a winner like my friends. I'll never be good enough to win prizes.

   b. I am not really good at sport. I just need to get over the fact that my friends are better at sport than I am.

   c. Ok, so I can't do cross country as well as my friends, but I am better than my friends at other things. I can win prizes that my friends can't.

   d. It's ok not to win prizes for everything and to not be great at everything. I don't mind when I don't win a prize and my friends do.

   e. Don't know.

10. There is a new student in the playground who makes other students say and do mean things and takes money off them. You find out you are sitting next to this bully on the bus on a school trip that you are really looking forward to. YOU THINK:

   a. Oh help! There is no way I can go on the trip now. I'm too scared. If I tell the teacher to move me, the bully will know and come and get me next time we're in the playground or on the way home from school. I'll never ever want to go into the playground again.

   b. I will be sick that day because I need to avoid the bully. In future I'll make sure to avoid them in the playground too.

   c. I will ask to sit beside a friend instead but I won't enjoy the trip because I know the bully will try to get me at some point.

   d. It would be unfair to miss my trip because of the bully. I will tell my teacher how I feel. Others will feel the same. The teacher will sit next to the bully and keep an eye on things so that I can enjoy the trip.

   e. Don't know.

ACTIVITY 3: THE WHAT HAPPENS NEXT GAME

1. It's your first day at the new school. You do not know anyone there. When you go to lunch, you are on your own.

What happens next?

2. The Maths teacher at your new school describes a new problem. Everybody is working away but you did not understand any of it.

What happens next?

3. You have been at your new school for a week now. It is very big, and you keep getting lost. One day you are late for class and don't know where you are.

What happens next?

4. You promised your new friend you would go to the cinema to see the latest block-buster but have fallen behind on your homework.

What happens next?

5. You have six exams in a row at the new school. You have been hanging out with your friends instead of studying. You need the grades.

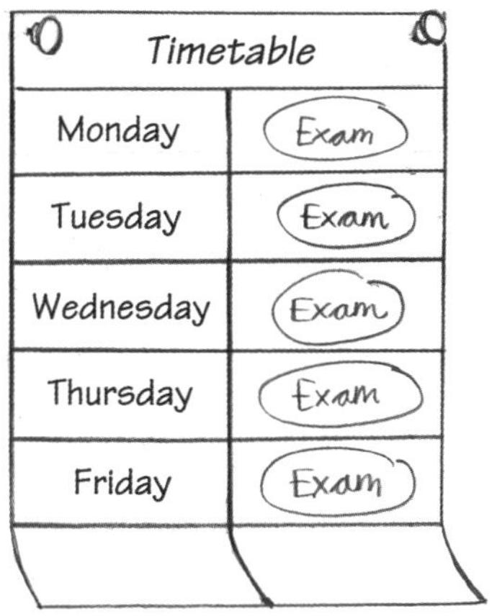

What happens next?

....

....

....

6. You have never liked speaking in public, but you have just found out that you need to do a speech for your class as part of the course.

What happens next?

....

....

....

7. You are with a crowd of friends when one of them pulls out some cigarettes. Some of the others light up. You want to say no but think they will laugh.

What happens next?

8. It's your second week at the new school and you still have not made any new friends. Everyone else seems to be in a group of their own.

What happens next?

9. You made a new friend who seems cool and funny. One day they tell you some of the others are planning to bunk school and wants you to come too.

What happens next?

....

....

....

10. A couple of older students at the new school have been saying mean things to you. One day they threaten you and take your money and packed lunch.

What happens next?

....

....

....

11. At the new school, a friend is having an all-night party. You don't want to feel left out by not going. Your parents say no because you are too young.

What happens next?

....

....

....

12. All of your new friends are chosen for a school sports team. You are not.

What happens next?

....

....

....

13. You don't like going on the school bus. The students can be annoying and rowdy and you can't 'walk away'.

What happens next?

....

....

....

14. You went to school wearing shoes that are not part of the school uniform. A teacher told you off. You got detention for saying, 'You can't tell me what to wear.'

What happens next?

....

....

....

15. One of your new teachers asks a question in class. You think you know the answer but feel too scared to put your hand up. You have been laughed at before for giving the wrong answer.

What happens next?

....

....

....

Online Resource Bank Contents List

Homunculi project templates

1. Skull
2. Thoughts and feelings screen
3. Gadget store
4. Traffic lights: Stop! Think! Do!
5. *Homunculi* character
6. Storyboard

Project admin documents for whole class/unit/group project

1. Info letter to parents template
2. Pupil participation permission template
3. Certificate of participation for pupils template
4. Invitation to awards event template

Lesson plan resources

Introductory webinars for professionals/ programme managers

References

Adegboye, D., Williams, F., Collishaw, S., Shelton, K., *et al.* (2021) 'Understanding why the COVID-19 pandemic-related lockdown increases mental health difficulties in vulnerable young children.' *Journal of Child Psychology and Psychiatry Advances*, 1(1), e12005.

Attwood, T. (2003) 'Cognitive Behaviour Therapy (CBT).' In L. Holliday Willey (ed.) *Asperger Syndrome in Adolescence: Living with the Ups and Downs and Things In Between.* London: Jessica Kingsley Publishers.

Baron-Cohen, S. (1992) 'The theory of mind hypothesis of autism: history and prospects of the idea.' *The Psychologist*, 5(1), 9–12.

Baron-Cohen, S. (2017) 'Editorial perspective: neurodiversity – a revolutionary concept for autism and psychiatry.' *Journal of Child Psychology and Psychiatry, and Allied Disciplines*, 58(6), 744–747.

Baron-Cohen, S., Ring, H., Williams, S., Wheelwright, S., *et al.* (1999) 'Social intelligence in the normal and autistic brain: a fMRI study.' *European Journal of Psychiatry*, 11(4), 1891–1898.

Beck, A. (1963) 'Thinking and depression: idiosyncratic content and cognitive distortions.' *Archives of General Psychiatry*, 9(4), 324–333.

Beck, A. (1976) *Cognitive Therapy and the Emotional Disorders.* New York: Meridian.

Briere, J. (1996) *Trauma Scales for Children and Adolescents (TSCC).* Lutz, FL: Psychological Assessment Resources (PAR).

British Psychological Society (2021) *Working with Autism: Best Practice Guidelines for Psychologists.* Leicester: BPS.

Currie, L. A. (1999) '"Mr Homunculus the Reading Detective": a cognitive approach to improving reading comprehension.' *Educational and Child Psychology*, 16(1), 37–42.

Demetriou, E. A., Lampit, A., Quintana, D. S., Naismith, S. L., *et al.* (2018) 'Autism spectrum disorders: a meta-analysis of executive function.' *Molecular Psychiatry*, 23(5), 1198–1204.

Drahota, A., Wood, J., Sze, K. & Van Dyke, M.' (2011) 'Effects of cognitive behavioral therapy on daily living skills in children with high-functioning autism and concurrent anxiety disorders.' *Journal of Autism and Developmental Disorders*, 41(3), 257–265.

Factor, R. S., Swain, D. M., Antezana, L., Muskett, A., *et al.* (2019) 'Teaching emotion regulation to children with autism spectrum disorder: outcomes of the Stress and Anger Management Program (STAMP).' *Bulletin of the Menninger Clinic*, 83(3), 235–258.

Flavell, J. H. (1979) 'Metacognition and cognitive monitoring: a new area of cognitive-developmental inquiry.' *American Psychologist*, 34(10), 906–911.

Fletcher-Watson, S. & Happé, F. (2019) *Autism: A New Introduction to Psychological Theory and Current Debate.* Oxford: Routledge.

Fonagy, P., Target, M., Cottrell, D., Phillips, J. & Kurtz, Z. (2002) *What Works for Whom?* London: Guilford Press.

Frith, U. (1989) *Autism: Explaining the Enigma.* Oxford: Blackwell.

Gaigg, S. B. (2012) 'The interplay between emotion and cognition in autism spectrum disorder: implications for developmental theory.' *Frontiers in Integrative Neuroscience*, 6, art. 113.

Gillot, A., Furniss, F. & Walter, A. (2001) 'Anxiety in high-functioning children with autism.' *Autism*, 5(3), 277–286.

Global Burden of Disease Collaborative Network (2022) *Global Burden of Disease Study 2019.* Seattle, WA: Institute for Health Metrics and Evaluation (IHME).

Gray, C. (2015) *The New Social Story Book: Revised and Expanded 15th Anniversary Edition.* Arlington, TX: Future Horizons.

Green, L., Gilchrist, A., Burton, D. & Cox, A. (2000) 'Social and psychiatric functioning in adolescents with Asperger Syndrome compared with conduct disorder.' *Journal of Autism and Developmental Disorders*, 30(4), 279–293.

Greig, A. & MacKay, T. (2005) 'Asperger's Syndrome and cognitive behaviour therapy: new applications for educational psychologists.' *Educational and Child Psychology*, 22(4), 4–15.

Greig, A., MacKay, T. & Nolan, A. (in preparation) 'Transition to secondary school: a whole-class *Homunculi* approach to reduce anxiety and build resilience for mainstream pupils including those with autism.'

Higginson, T. (1865) *The Works of Epictetus, Consisting of his Discourses in Four Books, the Enchiridion and Fragments. The Enchiridion, Section 5.* Boston, MA: Little, Brown and Co.

Hill, E. L. & Frith, U. (2003) Understanding autism: insights from mind and brain. *Philosophical Transactions of the Royal Society of London. Biological Sciences*, Series B, 358(1430), 281–289.

House of Commons Health and Social Care Committee (2021) *Children and Young People's Mental Health (HC17).* London: House of Commons.

Kanner, L. (1943) 'Autistic disturbances of affective contact.' *Nervous Child*, 2(1), 217–250.

Kapp, S. K., Gillespie-Lynch, K., Sherman, L. E. & Hutman, T. (2013) 'Deficit, difference, or both? autism and neurodiversity.' *Developmental Psychology*, 49(1), 59–71.

Kennedy, M., Coelho, C., Turkstra, L., Ylvisaker, M., *et al.* (2008) 'Intervention for executive functions after traumatic brain injury: a systematic review, meta-analysis and clinical recommendations.' *Neuropsychological Rehabilitation*, 18(3), 257–299.

Kreslins, A., Robertson, A. & Melville, C. (2015) 'The effectiveness of psychosocial interventions for anxiety in children and adolescents with autism spectrum disorder: a systematic review and meta-analysis.' *Child and Adolescent Psychiatry and Mental Health*, 9(1), 1–12.

Lai, M. C., Kassee, C., Besney, R., Bonato, S., *et al.* (2019) 'Prevalence of co-occurring mental health diagnoses in the autism population: a systematic review and meta-analysis.' *The Lancet Psychiatry*, 6(10), 819–829.

Lee, C. M., Cadigan, J. M., & Rhew, I. C. (2020) 'Increases in loneliness among young adults during the COVID-19 pandemic and association with increases in mental health problems.' *The Journal of Adolescent Health*, 67(5), 714–717.

MacKay, T. & Greig, A. (2008) 'The *Homunculi*: a cognitive behaviour therapy programme for young people with autistic spectrum disorders and other difficulties.' *The British Psychological Society Annual Conference 2008 Book of Abstracts*, 161–162.

MacKay, T., Knott, F. & Dunlop, A. (2007) 'Developing social interaction and understanding in individuals with autism spectrum disorder: a groupwork intervention.' *Journal of Intellectual and Developmental Disability*, 32(4), 279–290.

Mackenzie, E., McMaugh, A. & O'Sullivan, K. (2012) 'Perceptions of primary to secondary school transitions: challenge or threat?' *Issues in Educational Research*, 22(3), 298–314.

Marulis, L. M., Baker, S. T. and Whitebread, D. (2020) 'Integrating metacognition and executive function to enhance young children's perception of and agency in their learning.' *Early Childhood Research Quarterly*, 50, 46–54.

Moore, P. (1982) 'Children's metacognitive knowledge about reading: a selected review.' *Educational Research*, 24(2), 120–128.

National Institute for Health and Care Excellence (2013a) *Autism: The Management and Support of Children and Young People on the Autism Spectrum (Clinical Guideline 170).* London: NICE.

National Institute for Health and Care Excellence (2013b) *Social Anxiety Disorder: Recognition, Assessment and Treatment (Clinical Guideline 159).* London: NICE.

National Institute for Health and Care Excellence (2014) *Anxiety Disorders (Quality Standard 53).* London: NICE.

National Institute for Health and Care Excellence (2019) *Depression in Children and Young People: Identification and Management (Clinical Guideline 134).* London: NICE.

National Institute for Health and Care Excellence (2022) *Depression in Adults: Treatment and Management (Clinical Guideline 222).* London: NICE.

Newlove-Delgado, T., Williams, T., Robertson, K., McManus, S., *et al.* (2021) *Mental Health of Children and Young People in England, 2021: Wave 2 Follow Up to the 2017 Survey.* Leeds: NHS Digital.

Nuske, H. J. & Bavin, E. L. (2011) 'Narrative comprehension in 4–7-year-old children with autism: testing the Weak Central Coherence account.' *International Journal of Language & Communication Disorders*, 46(1), 108–119.

Ozonoff, S., Pennington, B. & Rogers, S. (1991) 'Executive function deficits in high functioning autistic children: relationship to theory of mind.' *Journal of Child Psychology and Psychiatry*, 32(7), 1081–1106.

Pellicano, E. (2010) 'Individual differences in executive function and central coherence predict developmental changes in theory of mind in autism.' *Developmental Psychology*, 46(2), 530–544.

Pellicano, E. & Burr, D. (2012) 'When the world becomes "too real": a Bayesian explanation of autistic perception.' *Trends in Cognitive Sciences*, 16(10), 504–510.

Perihan, C., Burke, M., Bowman-Perrott, L., Bicer, A., *et al.* (2020) 'Effects of cognitive behavioral therapy for reducing anxiety in children with high functioning ASD: a systematic review and meta-analysis.' *Journal of Autism and Developmental Disorders*, 50(6), 1958–1972.

Petersen, L. (1995) *Stop and Think Learning: A Teacher's Guide for Motivating Children to Learn, Including Those with Special Needs.* Victoria, Australia: ACER Press.

Powell, M. & Oei, T. (1991) 'Cognitive processes underlying the behavior change in cognitive behavior therapy with childhood disorders: a review of experimental evidence.' *Behavioural Psychotherapy*, 19(3), 247–265.

Radez, J., Reardon, T., Creswell, C., Orchard, F. & Waite, P. (2022) 'Adolescents' perceived barriers and facilitators to seeking and accessing professional help for anxiety and depressive disorders: a qualitative interview study.' *European Child and Adolescent Psychiatry*, 31, 891–907.

Rao, V., Mysore, A. & Raman, V. (2016) 'The neuropsychology of autism: a focus on three major theories.' *Journal of the Indian Association for Child and Adolescent Mental Health*, 12(2), 162–199.

Rice, F., Frederickson, N. & Seymour, J. (2011) 'Assessing pupil concerns about transition to secondary school.' *The British Journal of Educational Psychology*, 81(2), 244–263.

Rutter, M., Kim-Cohen, J. & Maughan, B. (2006) 'Continuities and discontinuities in psychopathology between childhood adult life.' *Journal of Child Psychology and Psychiatry*, 47(3/4), 276–295.

Seyfarth, R. M. & Cheney, D. L. (2013) 'Affiliation, empathy, and the origins of theory of mind.' *Proceedings of the National Academy of Sciences*, 110(Suppl. 2), 10349–10356.

Sharma, S., Hucker, A., Matthews, T., Grohmann, D. & Laws, K. R. (2021) 'Cognitive behavioural therapy for anxiety in children and young people on the autism spectrum: a systematic review and meta-analysis.' *BMC Psychology*, 9(1), 151.

Sherratt, D. & Peter, M. (2002) *Developing Play and Drama in Children with Autistic Spectrum Disorders.* London: David Fulton.

Sofronoff, K., Attwood, T., Hinton, S. & Levin, I. (2007) 'A randomized controlled trial of a cognitive behavioural intervention for anger management in children diagnosed with Asperger Syndrome.' *Journal of Autism and Developmental Disorders*, 37(7), 1203–1214.

Spence, S. (1995) *Social Skills Training: Enhancing Social Competence with Children and Adolescents.* Windsor: NFER-Nelson.

Spence, S., Barrett, P. & Turner, C. (2003) 'Psychometric properties of the Spence Children's Anxiety Scale with young adolescents.' *Anxiety Disorders*, 17, 605–625.

Stallard, P. (2002) 'Cognitive behaviour therapy with children and young people: a selective review of key issues.' *Behavioural and Cognitive Psychotherapy*, 30(3), 297–310.

Trevarthen, C. (1979) 'Communication and Co-operation in Early Infancy: A Description of Primary Intersubjectivity.' In M. Bullowa (ed.) *Before Speech: The Beginning of Human Communication.* London: Cambridge University Press.

Vrugt, A. & Oort, F. (2008) 'Metacognition, achievement goals, study strategies and academic achievement: pathways to achievement.' *Metacognition and Learning*, 3(2), 123–146.

Vygotsky, L. S. (1978) *Mind in Society: The Development of Higher Mental Processes.* Cambridge, MA: Harvard University Press.

Walęcka, M., Wojciechowska, K. & Wichniak, A. (2022) 'Central coherence in adults with a high-functioning autism spectrum disorder: in a search for a non-self-reporting screening tool.' *Applied Neuropsychology: Adult*, 29(4), 677–683.

White, J. (2020) *Supporting Children's Mental Health and Wellbeing at Transition from Primary to Secondary School: Evidence Review.* Edinburgh: NHS Health Scotland.

Wood, J. J., Kendall, P. C., Wood, K. S., Kerns, C. M., *et al.* (2020) 'Cognitive behavioral treatments for anxiety in children with autism spectrum disorder: a randomized clinical trial.' *JAMA Psychiatry*, 77(5), 474–483.

Index

additional support needs 87
Adegboye, D. 21
adults and *The Homunculi Approach* 86–7
affective theories 26
age ranges for *The Homunculi Approach* 86–7
agents in *The Homunculi Approach* 38–42, 55–6
  templates for 97
Attwood, T. 28

Baker, S.T. 27
Baron-Cohen, S. 24, 25
Barrett, P. 31
Bavin, E.L. 25
Beck, A. 24
Briere, J. 29
British Psychological Society 24

Cadigan, J.M. 21
central coherence 25
Cheney, D.L. 25
cognitive behaviour therapy (CBT) 24, 27–8
Currie, L.A. 23

Demetriou, E. A. 25
description of *The Homunculi Approach* 18–19
Drahota, A. 28

effectiveness of The Homunculi Approach 107
emotional, social and behavioural difficulties 20–1
engagement with *The Homunculi Approach* 84–5
Epictetus 24
evidence for *The Homunculi Approach*
  effectiveness of programme 29–31
  underlying principles 27–8
executive function 25

Factor, R.S. 27
final stages of *The Homunculi Approach* 63–70
Flavell, J.H. 27
focus on project 81
Fletcher-Watson, S. 25, 26
Fonagy, P. 27
Frederickson, N. 31
Frith, U. 25, 26
Furniss, F. 24

Gadget Store 44–5, 56, 98, 105
gadgets in *The Homunculi Approach* 38–9, 43–5, 55–7, 82
  templates for 98, 105
Gaigg, S.B. 26
generalising learning 83–4
Gillot, A. 24
Global Burden of Disease Collaborative Network 21
Gray, C. 28
Green, L. 24
Grieg, A. 27, 29, 31

Happé, F. 25, 26
Higginson, T. 24

Hill, E.L. 26
Homunculi Approach
  agents in 38–42, 55–6
  description of 18–19
  effectiveness of 107
  evidence for 26–31
  gadgets in 38–9, 43–5, 55–7, 82
  mission of 36–7
  missions in 38–9, 45, 55–61
  need for 20–1
  preparation for 46
  research into 88
  stages of 51–70
  start of 17–18
  theory behind 23–6
Homunculi template 102
House of Commons Health and Social Care Committee 21

'inappropriate' elements 84
initial stages of *The Homunculi Approach* 51–4

Kanner, L. 25, 26
Kapp, S.K. 24
Kennedy, M. 27
Kim-Cohen, J. 21
Kreslins, A. 27

Lai, M.C. 24, 27
learning difficulties 83, 85–6
Lee, C.M. 21
levels in Resource Bank 47–9

MacKay, T. 27, 29, 31
Mackenzie, E. 31
Marulis, L.M. 27
Maughan, B. 21
McMaugh, A. 31
Melville, C. 27
metacognition 23, 27
mission of *The Homunculi Approach* 36–7
missions in *The Homunculi Approach* 38–9, 45, 55–61
  templates for 96, 97
Moore, P. 23
Mysore, A. 26

National Institute for Health and Care Excellence 27, 28
need for *The Homunculi Approach* 20–1
neurodiversity 24–6, 85–6
Newlove-Delgado, T. 21
Nolan, A. 31
Nuske, H. 25

Oei, T. 24
Oort, F. 27
O'Sullivan, K. 31
Ozonoff, S. 25

parent/carer support 82, 83, 109–13
participant numbers 83
Pellicano, E. 25
Pennington, B. 25
Perihan, C. 27
Peter, M. 28
Petersen, L. 28
Powell, M. 24
preparation for *The Homunculi Approach* 46
primary to secondary transition project
  celebrating success 77
  class activities 126–44
  lesson plans for 114–25
  origins of 72–3
  outline of 71–80
  parental consent 109–13
  resources for 109–44
  teachers in 73–5

Radez, J. 21
Raman, V. 26
Rao, V. 26
research into *The Homunculi Approach* 88
Resource Bank levels 47–9
Rhew, I.C. 21
Rice, F. 31
Robertson, A. 27
Rogers, S. 25
role play 28
Rutter, M. 21

sample cartoons 92–4
Seyfarth, R. 25
Seymour, J. 31
Sharma, S. 27
Sherratt, D. 28
Skull poster 12, 19, 36, 37, 39–40, 43, 66–7, 103
Socratic Questioning 61, 74, 95
Sofronoff, K. 27
Spence Children's Anxiety Scale 31
Spence, S. 31

stages of *The Homunculi Approach*
creating agents, gadgets and missions 55–61
final stages 63–70
initial stages 51–4
Stallard, P. 27
start of *The Homunculi Approach* 17–18
Stop! Think! Do! Alarm 38, 43–4, 59, 106, 119
story records 99–101

theory behind *The Homunculi Approach*
cognitive behaviour therapy 24
metacognition 23
neurodiversity 24–6
theory of mind 25
Thoughts and Feelings Screens 19, 38, 43, 59–61, 68, 79, 80, 104
Trauma Symptom Checklist 29
Trevarthen, C. 26
Turner, C. 31

violent gadgets 82
Vrugt, A. 27
Vygotsky, L.S. 23

Walęcka, M. 25
Walter, A. 24
White, J. 71
Whitebread, D. 27
Wichniak, A. 25
Wojciechowska, K. 25
Wood, J.J. 27